Restoring The Image

An Introduction to
Christian
Counselling

by Roger F. Hurding
MA, MB, BChir, DRCOG
*Illustrated by the author
assisted by Bob Bond*

TO JOY

EXETER
THE PATERNOSTER PRESS

ISBN: 0 85364 268 0
Copyright © Roger Hurding 1980

AUSTRALIA
Emu Book Agencies Pty., Ltd.,
63 Berry Street, Granville, N.S.W., 2142

SOUTH AFRICA
Oxford University Press
P.O. Box 1141,
Cape Town

British Library Cataloguing in Publication Data

Hurding, Roger F
    Restoring the image.
    1. Pastoral counselling
    2. Peer counselling in the church
    I. Title
    253.5   BV4012.2

ISBN 0-85364-268-0

Typeset in 11pt Paladium by Photoprint, Paignton, Devon, and printed by Butler and Tanner Ltd., Frome, Somerset, for the Paternoster Press Limited, Paternoster House, 3 Mount Radford Crescent, Exeter, Devon.

Contents

Preface

Like many other Christian medical practitioners, I have been asked quite frequently to speak at conferences and evening meetings on some aspect of the vast subject of relationships. In so doing I have glimpsed something of the great hunger there is for clear, scriptural teaching and practical, caring advice in the complicated lives of countless men and women.

In January 1977 a series of five lectures, followed by discussion, was given to meet something of this need in the life of just one church in Bristol. About 100 people attended throughout and seemed to enjoy both the teaching material and the opportunity to react and discuss issues of personal importance. A further run of talks was given in the following June in the centre of Bristol to reach a wider Christian circle. There was a warm reception from Christians of many persuasions, including Brethren and Roman Catholics, as well as those from both charismatic and more traditional evangelical fellowships. The sense of oneness in Christ brought about in these discussions was encouraging to many of us.

It was soon seen that these five illustrated talks could be reproduced in a handbook, thus making the material available to others. I hope that the layout of the book, with discussion starters at the end of chapters two, three and four and with some advice on reading, will be useful for group study as well as for individuals who want to be more effective in their Christian caring.

I want also to make a disclaimer in this Preface. I realise that my brief allusions to Freudian psychoanalysis and Rogerian counselling in chapter one are open to misunderstanding and may look like a facetious dismissal of these important approaches to man's psychological needs. In fact, I believe that those of us involved in counselling and psychotherapy as Christians have a great deal to learn from the theories and practices of many others working in these fields. In this area there is a need for enlightened Christian evaluation of Gestalt therapy and Transactional Analysis, to mention just two approaches that have many devotees today. The aim of this book is in no way to exclude the valuable insights that such therapies can give, but rather to present certain key principles in caring for the psychological and emotional needs of others that are essentially scriptural. Whether you regard this goal as achieved or not, I would urge you to seek a continual openness to God's Word with respect to its theory and practice in all areas of human relationships.

I am grateful to a number of good friends who have encouraged me in the writing of this book — to the Revd. Paul Berg who was one of the first to see the possibilities of the handbook; to Janet Croysdale who has persisted with the tedious task of proof-reading; and most of all to Esme Nourse who, in the midst of a busy job as a vicar's secretary, has patiently typed her way through a forest of corrected and counter-corrected drafts. My special gratitude is towards my wife Joy and our three children, who have endured the vagaries of a distracted husband and father during these months of writing.

Roger F. Hurding

CHAPTER ONE

Principles of Christian Caring and Counselling

In this book we shall look at Christian caring with special emphasis on relationships — friend with friend, parent with child, husband with wife, fellow Christian with fellow Christian. We will consider what is commonly described as counselling. This is an easily misunderstood word and shortly I will attempt a working definition, as a basis for the book. I am concerned that we strike a balance between regarding counselling as only for the specially trained expert on the one hand, and on the other hand as something which anyone can do at 'the drop of a hat'.

THE NATURE OF MAN

Before we look at how to help others with their problems, it might be helpful to remind ourselves briefly what it means to be a human being. Our understanding of the nature of man is crucial as we try to help one another.

In Genesis 1 and 2 we read that God made man in his image and in his likeness; that he made man 'male and female'; and we understand from all this that man was a perfect whole, with three main aspects — mind, body and spirit. Thinking, feeling, creativity, intuition, doing, worshipping, relating and simply being were all beautifully integrated.

This diagram attempts to show the essential unity of man's

7

unfallen nature and, at the same time, suggests that this whole may be considered to be made up of three indivisible areas:

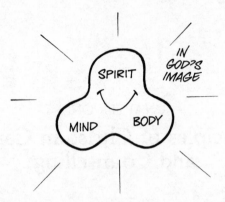

In Genesis 3 we see man's disobedience leading to shame and embarrassment, a guilty fear of the Lord God and blame-shifting. Remember how Adam blamed Eve and Eve blamed the serpent.

With the Fall the image of God in man was shattered and every aspect of man's being was distorted and spoilt:

Throughout the rest of history we see the fallenness of man in every part of his and her being.

Ephesians 4 is very helpful on this theme of counselling. In verses 18 and 19, Paul describes graphically the fallenness of the mind and spirit of man. "They are darkened in their understanding, alienated from the life of God because of the ignorance that is in them, due to their hardness of heart; they have become callous and have given themselves up to licentiousness, greedy to practise every kind of uncleanness". In Romans 7, Paul cries, "Who will deliver me from this body of death?" These and many other passages in both the Old and New Testaments remind us of what it means to live with the image of God broken.

Now, we all know how closely interwoven are the spiritual, the mental and the physical aspects of our life. We could take, say, a young man who is troubled by backache and he becomes more and more irritable with his girl friend. After some angry words with her he begins to feel guilty and even depressed. That night he is determined that he will begin to sort the whole thing out on his knees. As he gets down to pray, he finally slips his disc! We all know about this sort of experience. We become irritable when our bodies hurt, we lose our tempers with one another, we feel guilty and we may get depressed as a result. We may then try to pray and the pain may be too much for us. And so we see that there is an interconnectedness between mind, body and spirit; if there is trouble in one, there is trouble in the whole. This is shown diagrammatically in this next figure:

In this book we will concentrate particularly on psychological, emotional and spiritual aspects but we will not forget that we are dealing with the whole person.

There is one further point before we consider counselling in detail. Many Christians seem to be confused about the connection between *bodily* illness and a particular sin. Similarly, many Christians get confused about *psychological* problems and particular sins. In the Bible we see that in a general sense all sins relate to man's rebellion. The Bible also shows that physical disease is *sometimes* directly due to a person's sinning. It also shows that usually it is unrelated to that man's or woman's particular sins. Similarly, in the area of the mind, the Bible shows that the trouble is on certain occasions a result of sin. One example of this is found is Psalm 38 which has been described as one of the 'Psychosomatic Psalms'. Here, David says, "For my iniquities have gone over my head; they weigh like a burden too heavy for me. I am utterly spent and crushed; I groan because of the tumult of my heart". But in other situations in the Bible there is *no direct connection* between a particular sin and a person's mental troubles as with the suffering and depressed Job. So, throughout our contacts with people we need to ask from time to time: is this sadness, is it sickness or is it sin? If you like, putting it rather differently, is this person sad, mad or bad?

WHAT IS COUNSELLING?

Straightforwardly, to counsel is to advise. Immediately that conjures up to me pictures of the town council who are meant to advise us, although there is often more confusion than counsel in what they say! Some counselling gets a bit like that: the person we are trying to help ending up more confused following our advice. But there is a similar Latin word which has led to a different emphasis in today's English. From this we have the phrase 'to conciliate' or, more simply, 'to make friends with'. So we might put these two strands of meaning together and say that to counsel is to befriend, in order to advise or help someone.

WHAT IS THE AIM OF COUNSELLING?

What is the aim of this advising, of this befriending? Coming back to the picture of the shattered image of God in you and me, the Bible shows that the ultimate aim is that the image or likeness of God should be restored in us. For example, we read in 2 Corinthians 3:18, "And we all, with unveiled face, beholding the glory of the Lord, are being changed into his likeness from one degree of glory to another." By what means? Paul goes on, "For this comes from the Lord who is the Spirit." Paul speaks in more detailed language in Ephesians 4:11-16 which spells out the aim of counselling for us as Christians. Incidentally, I would recommend the study of this passage by all those who want to grow in Christian caring. In this section, Paul says that God gives us special gifts as Christians to work for him in the body of Christ. Why? In a word, he argues, for our *maturity*, as fully rounded, outgoing individuals, filled with the Spirit of Christ.

Can we be changed? The Bible tells us loud and clear that we can be! Our essential selves, our basic personalities, or in the Biblical language our 'old nature', are distorted, incomplete and sinful without Christ. By the nurture of the Holy Spirit, our new nature can develop. It is gradual, Paul tells us; it is a process, as he says, "from one degree of glory to another". But we need to see that this progression is never completed in this life. In other words, all that makes up the people we are is still influential once we become Christians and will continue, to some extent, to impede our progress. Eventually, of course, when we see Christ, the change is complete. We will be in his likeness, with the image of God restored! The next diagram illustrates this point:

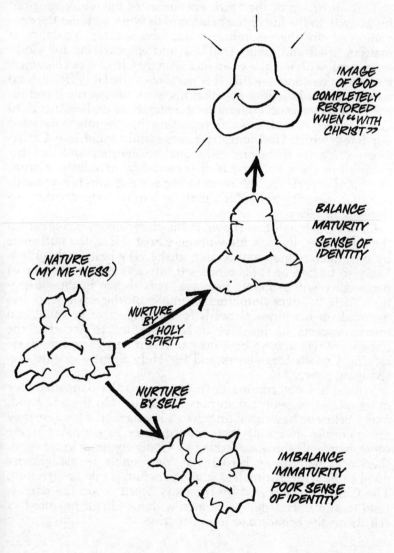

IMAGE OF GOD COMPLETELY RESTORED WHEN "WITH CHRIST"

BALANCE MATURITY SENSE OF IDENTITY

NATURE (MY ME-NESS)

NURTURE BY HOLY SPIRIT

NURTURE BY SELF

IMBALANCE IMMATURITY POOR SENSE OF IDENTITY

As you see from this diagram, we and those we try to help can move towards balance, maturity and a sense of identity, a sense of 'being me' in Christ. This can be effected only by the work of the Holy Spirit in our lives.

BELIEVER AND UNBELIEVER

This nurturing of the Spirit encompasses the whole range of his activity in the life of the believer. His work includes the conviction of sin, the assurance of our new sonship, guidance in matters small and great, enabling and empowering for God's service, all with the aim of an increasingly Christ-like character. However, we must see that this nurture of the Holy Spirit is no automatic road to glory and that his work necessarily dovetails with our repentance, commitment, receptivity and obedience to God's Word. Also, it is worth repeating that the raw material of our lives, which God longs to change and mould into Christlikeness, varies from one individual to another and that for many of us there are aspects of personality, heredity, environment and experience that seem to impede our progress towards spiritual maturity and which may be barely understood by us this side of glory.

On the other hand, as shown in the above diagram, we can go the other way, living a life without Christ. Here, the nurture is by our fallen human nature and, at the very best, such a life is likely to be one of enlightened self-interest. Any imbalance of personality will probably increase, as is shown in the illustration with its over-simplified example of the man who has majored on his physical needs to the neglect of spiritual and mental aspects of his life. It is important to see that the unbeliever will always be a prey to fallen desires and motives, lacking Christ's forgiveness and the Holy Spirit's specific life-changing power.

What I am *not* arguing in this section is that Christians are more attractive people than non-Christians. On the one hand, many believers have been drawn to a loving Christ because they are painfully aware of their inadequacies as people. On the other hand, all show something of God's common grace, and, therefore, many non-Christians are personable people who are good to be with. Ultimately, the distinction is one of direction. The Christian, nurtured by the Holy Spirit, is on the narrow road to glory. The man or woman without Christ, nurtured by self, is on the broad road to destruction.

THE IMPORTANCE OF LOVE

The growth in maturity which is the theme of this section is characterised by love. We may think of this self-giving love in three main areas: the love between God and ourselves, the love we have for our neighbour and fellow Christian, and the love we have for ourselves, or, using current expressions, self-acceptance and self-respect. John, in his first letter (1 John 4: 7-11, 19), shows the close connection between God's sacrificial love for us and our consequent love for him and for others. Jesus, in his two-fold summary of the commandments, points to the crucial link between the second and third areas of this love ("Love your neighbour AS YOURSELF.") The idea of loving oneself is frequently misunderstood by Christians, particularly when this concept is confused with self-centredness as the unattractive opposite of self-denial. However, we need to remember that the whole of the Bible teaches the worth of each individual, and that what God values enough to send his only son to redeem, we too should learn to value; in the last analysis, we insult God if we do not. For most of us the love of others inculcates and fosters our self-acceptance. Ideally, from the time of conception through birth, infancy, childhood, adolescence, and so to adult-hood, the love of family and friends builds up a healthy self-esteem. As we shall be reminded throughout the rest of this book, a great number of people lack this nurturing love and so find self-acceptance more difficult. For such, an awareness of God's unconditional love, often mediated through his people, may be the beginning of an increasing self-awareness and self-respect. A rightful self-acceptance growing out of right relationships does not preclude consciousness of weakness, failures and sin. In fact, the presence of God's love in our lives will encourage both the acceptance of the people we are, as made by God and redeemed through Christ, and the rejection of all that is unworthy of God's calling.

The first part of this next diagram shows how our self-esteem is built up by both God's love and the love of others. The second part shows how self-rejection cuts us off from this constructive two-way traffic of love, by denying that we are worthy of love from God, others and ourselves:

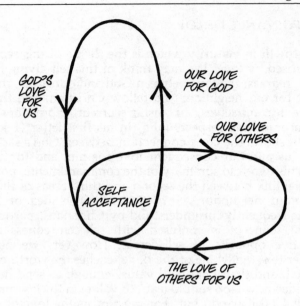

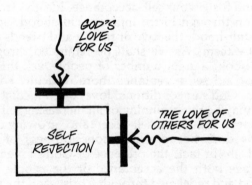

Paul says, "Who shall separate us from the love of Christ?"
To know that we are loved by God and to learn to love others
and ourselves as a result, leads to an increasingly strong sense of
identity so that we can say with conviction, "I am me". I
wonder if we can say that?

In our counselling, then, we need to remember this ultimate
aim of Christian maturity marked by love. In trying to help
other Christians with complex, unhappy and problematic relationships, or with inner fears, anxieties and guilt feelings, we
should be working towards a clearer understanding, more

loving attitudes and greater Christian maturity in their situations.

What about counselling non-Christians? I would suggest that at the very least our loving concern for them should show them that God too has a loving concern for them! It may be that the Holy Spirit will draw them to forgiveness and commitment to God in his good time so that his work of restoring the image of Christ can actually begin. It may be that such issues seem irrelevant to our non-Christian friends in their needs and then we must go on loving and caring, helping them to cope with life on their own terms, patiently and persistently. Whether counselling Christians or non-Christians, we shall see later that the principles are essentially the same. However, it is important to clarify one or two points on this matter of similarities and dissimilarities in counselling believers and non-believers.

Firstly, although the eventual goal of our counselling will be increasing Christian maturity, the more immediate aims will usually not be so exalted. If the Christian can be helped modestly forward on the road of God's will, then we should be thankful. If the non-Christian develops more responsible attitudes and better relationships as a result of our counselling, then we should be encouraged.

Secondly, we should see the relevance of the world-views of both the counsellor and the counsellee. Whether the counsellor sees the one he is trying to help as simply a higher animal, a sophisticated machine or as one of God's fallen image-bearers, the counselling situation will be coloured, sooner or later, by the counsellor's belief-system. Further, the world-view of the one being counselled, however sketchy that view may be, should always be respected. Where a Christian is counselling another Christian there will be a great deal of common ground and it is likely that, at some stage, the question of God's will, with regard to this situation or that relationship, will be considered. Although it may be right to challenge the presuppositions of the counsellee, there should always be a respect for his integrity and an attempt to encourage him to make adjustments and decisions on the basis of what he sees as responsible and appropriate. In helping others, it is easy to spend too little time in trying to understand the way they see themselves, others and the world in general.

WHO CAN COUNSEL?

As we consider this it may help us to look at this next diagram. This illustration greatly oversimplifies the issues but may nonetheless be useful for one or two points.

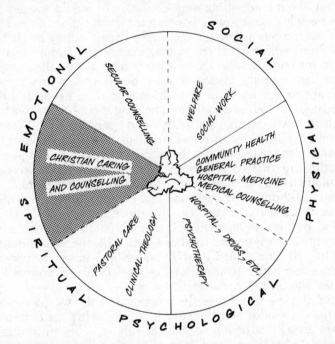

There right in the middle is our needy person, fallen from God's glory and surrounded by this great barrage of people who want to help. To be on the receiving end can be quite terrifying! You and I, as people who are caring Christians, have a certain section on this diagram but there are others trying to help. The fact that we are only one of so many individuals, teams and bodies who are caring and counselling should cut us down to size! On the other hand, the same fact may encourage us, in that we are not alone.

Who can counsel? Who can counsel with the sort of aims in mind that I have just described? I think that most of us feel unequal to the task.

Some people argue that counselling is one of God's special gifts to certain Christians and, as such, needs to be recognised and used in obedience to the Lord. Paul Morris, in his book *Love Therapy*, has this emphasis, quoting Romans 12:8. Here, a number of gifts that God gives the Church are mentioned, and Morris concludes that one of these gifts is the gift of counselling.[1] The RSV uses the word 'exhortation' but this can also be translated as 'encouragement' or 'the word of counsel'. Paul Morris balances his point by saying that the gift is widespread and is only known with certainty if one gets on with trying to counsel. Whether one believes that counselling is a special gift or not, this piece of advice makes sense.

Others reason that *all* Christians are called to counsel. Jay Adams in his book *Competent to Counsel* backs up this point by quoting Romans too;[2] he turns the pages to chapter 15:14 where Paul says, "I myself am satisfied about you, my brethren, that you yourselves are full of goodness, filled with all knowledge, and able to instruct one another." Adams sees these qualities as those of the counsellor and available for all Christians.

There is no doubt that the Psalms, Proverbs, Ecclesiastes, the Gospels and Epistles are full of instructions for believers on the life-long business of helping one another towards maturity. I suspect that the truth lies in *both* camps, that through God we can all be enabled to help one another but that he also especially equips certain of us in a ministry of counselling.

We can begin to come down to practicalities now.

WHAT QUALITIES ARE NEEDED?

What qualities are needed for counselling? Do we each need a diploma or a degree in Theology? Quick answer, "No!" Do we all need the expertise of psychiatric training? Quick answer, "No!" We may take encouragement from Jerome Frank, Professor of Psychiatry at John Hopkins University, who has written: "Anyone with a modicum of human warmth, common sense, some sensitivity of human problems and a desire to help can benefit many candidates for psychotherapy."[3] I think we can safely change the word 'psychotherapy' to 'counselling' in this statement. We should take heart that a great authority like Jerome Frank can point to such homely qualities as a basis for caring.

What is needed then, in more detail, to make us effective counsellors? First and foremost we must remember that one of the names of the Holy Spirit is Paraclete. This is from the Greek word which can be translated as Counsellor. Here the meaning is that of 'one summoned to the side of another', 'to befriend',

1. Morris, Paul D. *Love Therapy* (Coverdale, 1974) p. 16
2. Adams, Jay E. *Competent to Counsel* (Baker, 1970), p. 41
3. Frank, Jerome E. *Persuasion and Healing* (John Hopkins, 1973[2]) p. 167

'to advise' and 'if necessary, to plead his or her cause'. The Holy Spirit then is described as Counsellor — one who comes alongside to befriend. In counselling, all personal qualities and techniques must be, for the Christian, subordinate to the Holy Spirit. He is the one who changes the lives of both counsellor and counsellee. *If we want to counsel, we must be surrendered gladly to Christ and filled with the Holy Spirit day by day.* This, the Bible suggests, is fundamental. But nonetheless, what personal qualities will help us to be competent counsellors? Proverbs, Romans 12 and Ephesians 4 are specially helpful in answering this question. Try to study these passages, including the whole book of Proverbs if possible, in conjunction with this book.

Let us look now at some of the qualities needed for effective counselling.

EXPERIENCE OF AFFLICTION

The first requirement is experience of affliction. I am not asking you to go out and get afflicted — it us not up to me to advise you to do that! God loves us and allows adversity to strengthen our characters so that we can in turn help others. Paul describes this beautifully in 2 Corinthians 1:4. In the RSV the word 'comfort' is used. We read, "Blessed be the God and Father of our Lord Jesus Christ, the Father of mercies and God of all comfort (of all counsel, of all help) who comforts us in all our affliction, so that we may be able to comfort those who are in any affliction, with the comfort with which we ourselves are comforted by God." Paul is saying that God helps us in our affliction, so that we in turn may help others in their difficulties.

You will often find that those who seem to get alongside others to befriend and help have themselves been through a great deal of affliction and suffering. They know God's gracious strengthening and are in turn able to comfort others. There is a doctor in Bristol whose daughter was dying of leukaemia and he described how this Christian girl, knowing her pending death, radiated love and counsel to those around her. He said that one felt the better for visiting her. She had this experience of affliction and God's comfort, and so helped those with whom she came in touch. This refining through suffering often leads to the next quality that is required.

EMPATHY

Sympathy may say, "Oh, never mind dear, I feel really sorry

for you. Can I borrow your handkerchief?" Empathy may say nothing at all, but if it speaks, it talks like this: "It must be awful for you. I have listened to you and I am beginning to understand and feel with you in this." Empathy, this feeling *with*, this identification with somebody, is urged on us by Paul. In Romans 12:15 he says, "Rejoice with those who rejoice, weep with those who weep." The writer of Proverbs is more graphic, "He who sings songs to a heavy heart is like one who takes off a garment on a cold day and like vinegar in a wound" (Proverbs 25:20). Imagine your GP or your psychiatrist breaking into song over you as you come depressed into his consulting room! It would be as much a shock on the system as stripping off on a winter's day, says Proverbs, or splashing vinegar into a raw wound.

A GOOD LISTENER

We need to be good listeners. Have you experienced people that you want to share with or need help from and they *will not* listen to you? They may be silent but they are not with you. Their eyes are wandering around the room as you are talking; and, when they comment, you *know* that they have missed half of what you have said. One psychiatrist I know actually committed the 'unforgivable sin' of falling asleep while his patient went on, and on, and on. His listening powers had been sorely overtaxed.

Again, I wonder if you have had the experience when the person you have come to for help starts advising you long before you have told your story. Proverbs has it again (18:13), "If one gives answer before he hears, it is his folly and shame." I have found myself doing this, latching on to something said and then holding forth in a grand manner till I have caught the patient's eye, which seemed to say, "*Please* stop talking and listen to me!"

NON-JUDGMENTAL

This does not mean that we cannot make judgments about people but, being good listeners, we must give others a fair hearing. We should know our own frailty and weakness; it is part of our maturity to have this insight. Such self-knowledge should prevent us from jumping to conclusions or pointing the finger in an unloving way.

Job was nearly driven to despair by his judgmental so-called comforters. We see his distress, for example, in Job 19:1-3:

"Then Job answered, 'How long with you torment me, and break me in pieces with words? These ten times you have cast reproach upon me'. " Ten times! These men were quite relentless in their misguided counselling. Job continues, "Are you not ashamed to wrong me? And even if it be true that I have erred, my error remains with myself. If indeed you magnify yourselves against me, etc." That is exactly what they did. They magnified themselves against Job. These men judged. They thought they knew exactly what was wrong. And yet they were so wide of the mark that their advice was assault rather than counsel.

PERSISTENCE

It can be so easy to give up in our counselling. We seem to have been over the same ground endlessly and we can see no glimmer of improvement. It may well be right for both parties to give things a break for a while, but does our concern continue? Do we know something of Paul's persistence? In Colossians 1:28-29 we read, "Him (that is, Jesus) we proclaim, warning every man and teaching every man in all wisdom, that we may present every man mature in Christ. For this I toil, striving with all the energy which he mightily inspires within me." Again, we are reminded of the ultimate aim of counselling, Christian maturity. Notice the strong words — toil, striving, energy — that Paul uses to achieve this end. Do we persist?

There are many other qualities desirable for Christian caring. One only needs to describe the fruit of the Holy Spirit to give an ideal picture of the counsellor. However, the five qualities that I have mentioned are key ones in this area.

HOW DO WE COUNSEL?

There are endless theories about methods and techniques, based in turn on many different views of man. Freud's understanding of the mind has been very influential. His theories of our super-ego (or conscience), of our ego (or self) and of our id (or basic instincts), the use of the couch and the probings of psychoanalysis are tilted at in this song by Anna Russell, quoted by Jay Adams in *Competent to Counsel*.

I went to my psychiatrist to be psychoanalysed
To find out why I killed the cat and blacked my husband's eyes.
He laid me on a downy couch to see what he could find,
And here is what he dredged up from my subconscious mind:
When I was one, my Mummy hid my dolly in a trunk;

And so it follows naturally that I am always drunk.
When I was two, I saw my father kiss the maid one day,
And that is why I suffer now from kleptomania.
At three, I had the feeling of ambivalence towards my brothers,
And so it follows naturally I poison all my lovers.
But I am happy; now I've learnt the lesson this has taught;
That everything I do that's wrong is someone else's fault.[4]

Although the Psalmist said, "Commune with your own hearts on your beds, and be silent", I am not suggesting a sort of Christian counselling couch as part of our equipment for caring! Psychoanalysis may have its place for the trained expert but such deep and protracted delving into the psyche cannot be part of our approach as lay counsellors.

Others may have come across non-directive counselling, which is a method widely used by many, including marriage guidance counsellors. Carl Rogers is the key name in this approach. Jay Adams gives an example of this technique which, though it may be a little unfair, does show the weakness of this approach in its pure form. In this scene we have the counsellor and someone in need.

"The client begins the interview: 'I'm really upset.' The counsellor focuses upon that word and reflects it back in different words: 'I see that you're torn two ways.' 'That's right', says the client, 'I'm very distressed.'
'I see,' the counsellor replies, 'that you are quite troubled.'
'My difficulty is that I don't know what to do about a certain problem,' says the client.
'You are trying to find a solution,' says the counsellor.
'Yes, that's right. I've had a problem with homosexuality. Do you think homosexuality is wrong?' asks the client.
And his counsellor replies, 'I see you are asking me whether homosexuality is ethically or religiously proper'. "[5]

Jay Adams likens this parrot-like repetition of what the counsellee says to being more like 'a parakeet that a paraclete![6] Paul D. Morris in *Love Therapy* is more positive in his comments on non-directive counselling and says that 'it helps the client to help himself'.[7]

This helpful approach encourages the client to identify prob-

4. Adams, Jay E. op. cit. p. 8
5. Adams, Jay E. op. cit. p. 91
6. Adams, Jay E. op. cit. p. 84
7. Morris, Paul D. op. cit. p. 39

lems, perhaps in a new light, and then to establish what are the alternative courses of action open to him or her.

I have mentioned Jay Adams several times now and I would like to say a little about his book *Competent to Counsel*, which some of you may have read. Although there are some very helpful sections in this book and some stimulating insights, I cannot recommend it unequivocally. As you may know, he and his colleagues practise what they call nouthetic counselling, based in the New Testament Greek word which is commonly translated as 'teach' or 'admonish'. He argues that all so-called 'mental illness' can be traced to specific sin or sins.[8] I would suggest that the biblical view of the Fall of man does not support his theory and I have indicated that earlier in this chapter. Incidentally, Jay Adams concludes that psychiatry is therefore spurious; if there are no psychological illnesses then there is no need for pyschological doctors.[9]

We have been cautious about the psychoanalyst's couch, about completely non-directive counselling and the rather narrow framework of Jay Adams' nouthetic counselling. What is there left? What principles should we keep in mind in counselling and what are the more important pitfalls? Another American, Dr. William Glasser, practises what he calls Reality Therapy. In his approach he uses three principles, which I believe are in accord with the biblical view of man. The first of these is *involvement*.

INVOLVEMENT

There are many therapists and counsellors who believe profoundly in non-involvement and complete detachment. Try as he or she might, the person who is being counselled cannot elicit a flicker of response from the expressionless face or voice of the counsellor. Try and shock him and nothing happens. Tell him a dreadful story and he just looks impassively at you. Now, although I agree with the picture of the counsellor being a sounding board off which the person being helped can bounce their comments, in order to sort out their difficulties for themselves, I do not see that the counsellor should behave like an inanimate sounding board in all respects!

We have already seen that the 'Paraclete' signifies the way in which the Holy Spirit is called alongside to befriend and help. The Holy Spirit could not be *more* involved with us and those we try to help, if we will let him. Interestingly, the same word 'para-

8. Adams, Jay E. op. cit. p. 28, 29
9. Adams, Jay E. op. cit. p. 36, 37

clete' is used in a number of places in the New Testament, (e.g. Romans 12:6-8) for the Christian who has a counselling ministry.

We too then need to be *involved* in our Christian caring. What does this mean in terms of time and the nature of the encounter?

Firstly, let us consider the time factor. We must be balanced and disciplined about this. Most of us lead busy lives and counselling will be one of many responsibilities. Although our Lord was readily available to people at all hours, we forget that he took 30 years of domestic commitment to prepare for his ministry. And even then he needed times of withdrawal and relaxing friendship during his two to three years of special work. We too need a right perspective in our availability to those in need. There may be times when we are called on in a crisis situation. If this is the case and we are not available, then communication in the body of Christ should be good enough for a little telephoning to produce someone who *can* help. So often the crisis is *not* as urgent as it at first seems and a day or two's delay may help all round! Generally, we will be more wise to offer time on a reasonable basis. Half an hour of concentrated discussion will be more helpful than long hours of soul-searching into the small hours of the morning.

Secondly, what about the nature of the encounter between you and the person you are trying to help? Very often our counselling will be on a one to one basis. We have excellent examples in our Lord's encounters with Nicodemus, the woman at the well, Simon Peter after the Resurrection, and so on. Particularly in marriage counselling (see chapters four and five) we may well be involved with two individuals at once.

In psychiatry another important mode of encounter is the group. There is no space to look at this thoroughly but it is worth pointing out that house groups and house fellowships can be an important part of Christian caring and can bring healing. It may be that a group will develop a constructive identity of its own, within which people can learn to share, to be honest, to love and be loved. The spokes of a wheel are nearest to one another when they are nearest to the centre. Such Christ-centred groups will experience this increasing unity in love.

In our involvement, what are some of the pitfalls that we need to look out for?

Dependency

Here is a real danger! We all love to feel wanted, including the counsellor. It can give a nice, cosy feeling inside to see that someone is responding to our help. We may find ourselves thinking, "So many others have tried to help this person and *at last* he or she has managed to track *me* down." Now here there should be a warning sign for both the counsellor and the counsellee. The counsellee, the person being helped, leans more and more on the counsellor in a demanding and possessive way. At first, the counsellor may welcome this flattering attention but at some point or other the whole thing turns sour and both individuals are the worse off. They remembered that Christians should have an 'open door' to others but they forgot that open doors should also have a bolt on the inside! In the end the counsellor feels of the counsellee that: "People who want by the yard but try by the inch should be kicked by the foot."

Our aim in counselling is to encourage towards Christian maturity, and one of the marks of maturity is a degree of independence. Better still is the idea of inter-dependence, where people have some sense of inner harmony and at the same time are learning to share with others. The diagrams shown on page 27 illustrate the way a counsellor can help a fellow-Christian, who is not coping, towards increased interdependence. With this aim in view we can describe the counsellor as catalyst, communicator and conciliator. He is *a catalyst* in that his help should stimulate the counsellee towards personal growth; he is *a communicator* in that he should encourage the person being helped to see more clearly his situation, and he is *a conciliator* in that he will be instrumental in helping the non-coper towards improved relationships.

Shopping Around

Another pitfall is 'shopping around'. This can be as equally unproductive as the exclusiveness of dependence. We all know the situation. A has a problem and he or she talks about this at every opportunity. Soon B, C, D and E are *all* involved with varying degrees of enthusiasm, each feeling that he or she is *the* problem-solver in this situation. One day D becomes uneasy when, after getting some well thought-out advice, A says, "That's not what B says" and then, later in the conversation, "C says I ought to do the exact opposite to what you say." Everyone is trapped. B, C, D and E are probably wasting their time and A is no nearer to solving his or her problem, secure amidst so much contrary advice.

If you find yourself in this situation, I suggest that you need to challenge A by asking whether he or she really wants a solution; and if so, A must try to see it through with either B, C, D *or* E. It may be that in time A will find more help from F or G but at least there has been persistent and loving involvement to try to see the thing through.

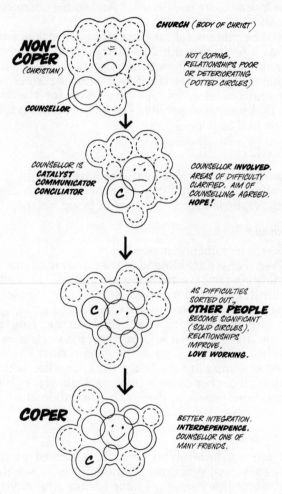

NON-COPER (CHRISTIAN)

COUNSELLOR

CHURCH (BODY OF CHRIST)

NOT COPING, RELATIONSHIPS POOR OR DETERIORATING (DOTTED CIRCLES)

COUNSELLOR IS **CATALYST COMMUNICATOR CONCILIATOR**

COUNSELLOR **INVOLVED**, AREAS OF DIFFICULTY CLARIFIED, AIM OF COUNSELLING AGREED. **HOPE!**

AS DIFFICULTIES SORTED OUT, **OTHER PEOPLE** BECOME SIGNIFICANT (SOLID CIRCLES). RELATIONSHIPS IMPROVE, **LOVE WORKING.**

COPER

BETTER INTEGRATION. **INTERDEPENDENCE.** COUNSELLOR ONE OF MANY FRIENDS.

Confidentiality

The third pitfall is the failure to observe confidentiality. This is an extension of the 'shopping around' problem, and I believe that a lack of respect for confidentiality is very disruptive in the life of the body of Christ. Again, it is easy to be trapped. Often it is the fault of both parties.

A has bared his or her soul to B and then the next week tells C his or her life story. C meets B in the street. "By the way," says C, "A came to see me yesterday. Sad story, isn't it? Did you know that A was involved with X?" B replies, "Well, *I* understood that Y was more important." And so the sorry conversation goes on.

Beware! The Bible is full of warnings against idle words. Let Proverbs 25:9 serve to remind us, "Argue your case with your neighbour himself, and do not disclose another's secret."

If in counselling you see the desirability of further consultation with someone else, ask A's permission for you to chat it over with that particular person. The whole matter is ultimately one of trust and loyalty.

RESPONSIBILITY

In thinking about involvement, we have thought too about the counsellor's responsibility. Let us now consider the matter of evoking responsibility *in the person being helped.*

It's Grandma's Fault

As we listen to someone in need, it is easy to be so concerned and involved that we are blinded to the question of that person's responsibility. In fact, we are being too gullible. This attitude of mind is mentioned in Proverbs 14:15, "The simple believes everything but the prudent looks where he is going." We can end up by saying something like this: "I see that you can't help the way you are. I see that all your problems relate to the fact that Grandma locked you up in the garden shed."

We *must* at some stage challenge the counsellee with the *responsibility* of his or her own resentment, jealousy, or bitterness. Repentance, forgiveness and growth towards maturity are all available in Christ.

Inner Healing

I must write a little about what is described as the inner healing of emotional problems. Although I have not thought a great deal about this concept, I have friends who have found a measure of peace through this approach.

Francis MacNutt in his compassionate book *Healing* has a helpful chapter on inner healing. He suggests that prayer for inner healing is appropriate where 'powerful memories of the past rise to fill us with fear and anxiety, whether we wish these fears or not. We cannot wish them away by an act of will'.[10]

10. Macnutt, Francis. *Healing*, (Ave Maria Press, 1974) p. 183

He says that inner healing involves two things:

(i) Bringing to light the things that hurt us. Usually this is best done with another person; even the talking out of the problem is in itself a healing process.

(ii) Praying to the Lord to heal the binding effects of the hurtful incidents of the past.

Don't bite off more than you can chew

Here is a difficult area. Some of the folk who come to us may be in desperate need; they may be chronically alcoholic or on the point of suicide, for example. Their problems are such that they may need the special help of such bodies as Alcoholics Anonymous or the Samaritans; or alternatively they may need psychiatric help.

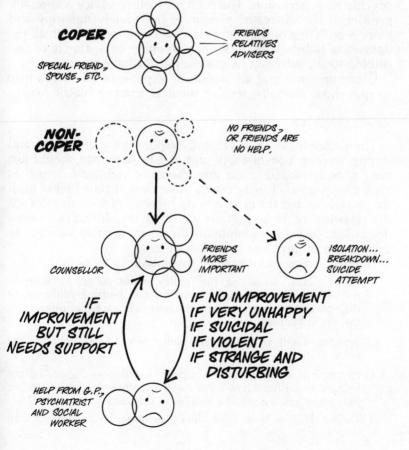

COPER

SPECIAL FRIEND, SPOUSE, ETC.

FRIENDS RELATIVES ADVISERS

NON-COPER

NO FRIENDS, OR FRIENDS ARE NO HELP,

COUNSELLOR

FRIENDS MORE IMPORTANT

ISOLATION... BREAKDOWN... SUICIDE ATTEMPT

IF IMPROVEMENT BUT STILL NEEDS SUPPORT

IF NO IMPROVEMENT
IF VERY UNHAPPY
IF SUICIDAL
IF VIOLENT
IF STRANGE AND DISTURBING

HELP FROM G.P., PSYCHIATRIST AND SOCIAL WORKER

The diagram on page 29 illustrates how the 'non-coper' may need not only the help of the counsellor but also that of the general practitioner, psychiatrist and the whole range of social services.

It cannot be part of this book to give details of mental illness. There have been many attempts at quick, easy definitions, such as, "A psychotic is someone who adds 2 plus 2 and gets 5; and a neurotic is someone who adds 2 plus 2 and gets 4, but is unhappy about it." Some of the books mentioned at the end of this book will be more helpful in this area than this slim statement!

Nonetheless, we should encourage our more disturbed friends to see someone with the appropriate special training and experience. This may be a minister or other Christian leader, the general practitioner or specialist if they are already under psychiatric supervision. The need for further advice is specially pressing if the distressed person is: desperately unhappy and there is no lifting of the depression; suicidal; violent with all the dangers of baby-, wife- or granny-bashing; or is strange or disturbing to us, suffering from delusions or hallucinations.

Common-sense and an increasing experience will often help us spot those specially needing medical and psychiatric help.

RIGHT AND WRONG

The principles of involvement, responsibility and 'right and wrong' overlap considerably and as Christians we should not need to be reminded of the importance of 'right and wrong' as we try to counsel. It may take a great deal of time before both the counsellor and the person being helped can see how relevant the question of right and wrong is in the difficulties under discussion. Just one example of this dilemma must suffice, the quite common problem of guilt feelings.

Harold Darling has described three main types of guilt:[11]

(i) Social Guilt, when we feel guilty about social injustice in relation to such issues as the Arms Race, housing problems or the contrast between our comparative affluence and poverty in the Third World;

(ii) Spiritual Guilt where we are guilty before God, whether we know it or not;

(iii) Psychological Guilt which Tournier describes as due to "failure to dare to be ourselves". We have already seen the possibility that inner healing may be helpful in this area.

11. Darling, H. *Man in his Right Mind* (Paternoster Press, 1969) pp. 53ff.

Although anxiety is a dread of the future, guilt is a dread of the past. This series of diagrams may help us to see how true spiritual guilt may be dealt with in four different ways by the person in need. The illustrations show the guilty person in tripartite shape, reminding us of the broken image of God, in mind, body and spirit.

DEPRESSION

Here we see a sensitive and introverted person who has allowed the burden of guilt to weigh him or her down into a state of depression.

REPRESSION

Here there has been an attempt to bury guilt, to 'sweep it under the carpet' or simply to forget it. This way of repression was the one that Adam and Eve took when they hid guiltily from the Lord God among the trees of the garden. Instead of saying, "God, we have done wrong. Please help us!", there was blame-shifting from Adam to Eve and so to the serpent. This dishonesty led to the repression of guilt and the sorry tale continued.

OBSESSION

Here is another inward-looking person who revels in morbid thoughts. He or she becomes preoccupied with guilt, saying, "I

have done this and that; I am guilty; I am much too bad for anyone, including God, ever to forgive." This sort of person
wallows in a mire of self-recrimination, and sometimes enjoys
it!

CONFESSION

The fourth way of dealing with guilt is confession, or
'exteriorising the rottenness' as William James put it. In our
counselling we may at times be able to help people to an understanding of personal guilt. This opens the way to confession,
making amends and so to the peace of forgiveness and a new
beginning. It is important to see that Christian caring may
include the need to admit personal blame to another as well as
to God himself. Matthew 5:23-24 is one of a number of passages
that urge the need of restitution, "First be reconciled to your
brother" is the command.

It is essential when counselling to be especially sensitive and
compassionate in this area of right and wrong. There is a great
danger for Christians, with a list of ready texts at hand, to jump
to hasty conclusions. The situations that people get into are
rarely that simple and we need a great deal of loving empathy as
we bear with the counsellee in his or her dilemmas. Quite often
the person in difficulty faces difficult choices, where every
course of action seems to be the sad outcome of wrong decisions
and disrupted relationships. The counsellor must never be judgmental and yet it may be his responsibility to help the counsellee
disentangle the complex skeins of psychological guilt and guilt
before the Lord God.

CONCLUSION

Let me conclude this chapter on the principles of Christian
caring by the reminder that counselling is *not* just a question of
method and technique although these are important. As
Christians we know that "Christ takes 'nobodies' and makes
'somebodies' ". It is helpful to remember two key aspects of this
glorious truth.

Firstly, it is the Holy Spirit who can change our personalities towards that maturity which we have seen is the ultimate aim of counselling. In 2 Corinthians 3:18 we read: "And we all, with unveiled face, beholding the glory of the Lord, *are being changed into his likeness* from one degree of glory to another; for this comes from the Lord who is the Spirit."

Secondly and finally, our counselling must be based on scriptural principles, for the Bible is given to stimulate our growth towards the same maturity and completeness. This point is clearly made in 2 Timothy 3:16, 17: "All scripture is inspired by God and profitable for teaching, for reproof, for correction, and for training in righteousness, *that the man of God may be complete*, equipped for every good work."

FOR FURTHER READING

Darling, H. *Man in his Right Mind* (Exeter, The Paternoster Press) 1970

Fowkes, R. *Coping with Crises* (London, Hodder & Stoughton) 1968

Hoekema, A. A. *The Christian Looks at Himself* (Eerdmans) 1975

Kidney, D. *The Book of Proverbs* (Tyndale Commentary, Leicester, IVP) 1964

Macaulay, R. and Barrs, J. *Christianity with a Human Face* (IVP) 1979

Mobbs, B. *Our Rebel Emotions* (London, Hodder & Stoughton) 1970

Trobisch, W. *Love Yourself* (Editions Trobisch) 1976

CHAPTER TWO
Counselling Adolescents

"This youth is rotten from the bottom of their hearts; the young people are malicious and lazy; they will never be as youth happened to be before; our today's youth will not be able to maintain our culture."

This statement is not from the pen of a modern moralist but was written on clay and found in the ruins of Old Babylon, dated at more than 3,000 years ago.

Adolescents have always had a bad press from adults with short memories and I hope that in this chapter we will be able to redress the balance. If we are to counsel adolescents we must have an understanding of adolescence.

WHAT IS ADOLESCENCE?

The Shorter Oxford English Dictionary defines adolescence as: 'The process of growing up; the period between childhood and maturity.' Many other definitions have been offered. For example, adolescence has also been called 'Age Between' and 'a pilot experiment in independent living.'

Apart from infancy, it is the period of greatest growth and development in the life of the individual. For many, the voyage to adulthood is a comparatively calm one; for many it is a time of painful adjustment; and for a few the 'In-Between' years are ones of disruption and crisis.

STAGES OF ADOLESCENCE

Although the age limits of adolescence are difficult to define, it may help to think of three main stages of development between childhood and adulthood:

EARLY ADOLESCENCE

Early adolescence lasts for about three years, from the age of 11 or 12 to 14 or 15 and is the period of *puberty*. This word is here used to describe those biological changes that take place in the young person leading to increasing sexual awareness.

General

This awakening interest in sex may be first noticed in the family where boys of, say 11, will become preoccupied by the sexuality of their mothers, perhaps attempting to touch their breasts and saying things like, "My Mum's my girl-friend."

Similarly, girls may become more feminine and seductive towards their fathers and may say, "When I grow up, I'll marry Dad!"

Early adolescence is also a time of emotional withdrawal where parents find themselves saying repeatedly, "Are you deaf?" and the young teenager may turn away irritably, exclaiming, "Leave me alone!"

This feeling is beautifully expressed in an adolescent's simple prayer in *You must be joking, Lord* by Michael Hollings and Etta Gullick:

> "Lord, I find it much easier to love my cat than my mother; give me balance, Lord."[1]

Further, there is need for physical withdrawal as the young person begins to adjust to his or her changing body. Here is the time when privacy in the bathroom should be respected and, if possible, a separate bedroom should by now be an established part of life.

Boys

In early adolescence, other boys are specially important. This is the time when the more boisterous may form warlike gangs and the more sensitive may form secret societies and other in-groups. There may be hot competition at sport or study but less acceptable to adults is the way such groups may compare their prowess at spitting, urinating or ejaculating.

Further, as boys develop they find girls increasingly interesting. Life can be a mixture of heaven and hell as attraction and embarrassment go hand-in-hand. This terrible dilemma is crystallized in Adrian Henri's *Song for a Beautiful Girl Petrol-Pump Attendant on the Motorway:*

> 'I wanted your soft verges
> But you gave me the hard shoulder.'[2]

1. Hollings, Michael and Gullick, Etta. *You Must Be Joking, Lord* (Mayhew-McCrimmon, 1975) p. 92
2. Henri, Adrian, *Penguin Modern Poets* 10, (Penguin Books, 1967) p. 20

To make it all worse, boys grow more rapidly than girls and the 'hell' side of it is often made worse by clumsiness. It is an age of bumping into things and feeling in the way.

Along with vivid sexual dreams and waking wet from ejaculating, masturbation is a feature of life than can be pre-occupying in early adolescence, for both boys and girls. Some take this in their stride, others feel guilty and a few may be obsessed and greatly upset by the habit. Although in the past many Christians have given dire warnings about masturbation, it is fair to say that there are no scriptural grounds for such an attitude. Rather we should advise that as an occasional release of sexual tension it is not wrong, although masturbation is a pale shadow of real love-making, which may be part of God's plan for the young person later in life.

Girls

While their male contemporaries are banging into doors and tripping up curbs, girls seem to be less clumsy due to a slower rate of growth. Once their growth spurt is over, periods often start and breast development becomes more obvious.

Girls of this age are inclined to form one to one relationships with each other. Whereas the early adolescent boy tests out his masculinity with other boys, girls in their early teens need other males to be assured of their femininity. This may be a young male teacher or friend of the family. These diagrams illustrate this difference between the early adolescent boy and girl:

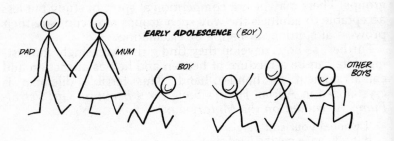

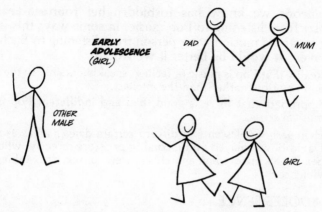

EARLY ADOLESCENCE (GIRL)

DAD

MUM

OTHER MALE

GIRL

It is not unusual for a girl in her early teens to have a fantasy hero with whom she can have an idealised love affair in her imagination.

Occasionally this make-believe can persist unheathily, making normal friendships with other young men a problem. I can still remember a young woman who was fantasising about a pop star in an intensive way at the age of 19 and 20. The singer in question was especially popular in her early teens and yet, seven years or so later, she still believed that she was in love with him, much to the frustration of her would-be boy-friend.

This is perhaps a good place to say something briefly about Pop music. Many of us as parents of teenagers or even runners of school discos, can feel very threatened by Pop, mainly because we find it shocks our senses and we cannot understand it. Someone we know has forbidden her fourteen-year-old daughter from listening to Pop music. In some ways this is like trying to stop a music-loving person from listening to Bach and Beethoven. It would be better if we would:

(i) Realise that Pop is music of feeling, speaking mainly to the body and emotions rather than the intellect.

(ii) Appreciate that there is good, bad and indifferent Pop in the musical sense.

(iii) Help early adolescents to discern certain danger areas as when David Bowie played on bisexuality or, more recently, when the Sex Pistols majored on anarchistic views of sex, drug-taking and violence.[3]

MID-ADOLESCENCE

Mid-adolescence lasts for about another three years from the age of fourteen or fifteen to seventeen or eighteen and is the period of *identification*, i.e. beginning to discover one's identity. Eric Erikson defined identity as 'a conscious sense of individual uniqueness'. We might more simply say, "An ability to feel 'I am me' or 'this is what I am' ".

There are many aspects that contribute to the growing sense of identity of the young person in his or her teens and we shall look at the more important factors a little later.

This search for significance rightly involves a great deal of questioning on the imponderables of life — pain, disease, poverty, earthquakes and train crashes. This frame of mind is seen in the prayer *You must be joking, Lord:*

"The news of Jesus Christ says: Peace on earth.
The news of the world says: War in the Middle East.
The news of Jesus Christ says: Peace to men of goodwill.
The BBC says: Fifty Buddhist monks have been slaughtered.
The news of Jesus Christ says: The meek shall inherit the earth.
The Telstar programme is highlighting exploitation of the poor in Latin America . . ."[4]

If the home is a loving and reasonably secure one, then the mid-adolescent stands quite a good chance of resolving many of these conflicts. This may be the age of some very important decisions concerning the future and with regard to what is believed or disbelieved. Fifteen was the age when my own Christian commitment hesitantly began.

3. Graham Cray has written a useful chapter on Pop music in *Time to Listen, Time to Talk* (Falcon, 1974) by John and Moyra Prince. My comments are an echo of his.

4. Hollings, Michael and Gullick, Etta op. cit. p. 16

Nonetheless, this is also the age group of the so-called Generation Gap. It is a time of life when one may need to test everything out: parents, school, police, government and indeed every form of authority. Those of us with children know that this opposition may start much earlier! When our elder daughter, Sarah, was six and three-quarters and sent to her bedroom over a dispute with my wife, Joy, she was later found packing her case! Challenged by Joy, Sarah replied, "There are two problems in my life: Mrs. Rees, the headmistress, and you! Anyway, the Bible says that I should obey God, not you!" Fortunately, Joy remembered the Fifth Commandment in time and the case was duly unpacked. If the more important parts of one's environment stand up to the testing out of mid-adolescence, then this phase will often last for only six months or so. If the surroundings are found wanting and the young person's own sense of identity is elusive as a result, then there may be bigger trouble. Depending on the nature of what one is rejecting, there may be many different routes chosen:

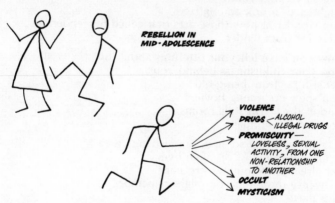

REBELLION IN MID-ADOLESCENCE

VIOLENCE
DRUGS — ALCOHOL / ILLEGAL DRUGS
PROMISCUITY — LOVELESS, SEXUAL ACTIVITY, FROM ONE NON-RELATIONSHIP TO ANOTHER
OCCULT
MYSTICISM

These are areas that are easily sensationalised and we need to look at our own adult lives before leaping to swift condemnation. Kenneth Leech's book *Youthquake* helpfully documents this explosion of 'escape routes'.

Shakespeare said this of adolescence in his *Winter's Tale* (Act III, scene 3):

"I would there were no age between ten and three and twenty, or that youth would sleep out the rest; for there is nothing in the between but getting wenches with child, wronging the ancientry, stealing, fighting. Hark you now! Would any but these boiled brains of nineteen and two and twenty hunt this weather?"

We are reminded that 'getting wenches with child' is no new characteristic of mid- and late adolescence, although in this day of free contraception and readily available abortion some people seem to feel that the issues are nicely buttoned up. A generalisation sometimes made about these years of development is, 'Whereas boys want sex, girls want love'. This poem by Brian Patten illustrates these different expectations:

Portrait of a Young Girl raped at a Suburban Party

After this quick bash in the dark
You will rise and go
Thinking of how empty you have grown
And of whether all the evening's care in front of mirrors
And the younger boys disowned
Led simply to this.

Confined to what you are expected to be
By what you are
Out in this frozen garden
You shiver and vomit —
Frightened, drunk among trees,
You wonder at how those acts that called for tenderness
Were far from tender.

Now you have left your titterings about love
And your childishness behind you
Yet still far from being old
You spew up among flowers
And in the warm stale rooms
The party continues.

It seems you saw some use in moving away
From that group of drunken lives
Yet already ten minutes pregnant
In twenty thousand you might remember
This party
This dull Saturday evening
When planets rolled out of your eyes
And splashed down into suburban grasses.[5]

LATE ADOLESCENCE

Lasting from the age of seventeen or eighteen to the early twenties we can describe late adolescence as the period of *coping*. Where young people leave school early and enter jobs quickly, mid- and late adolescence fuse together. They have to if the late teenager is to cope with his new-found responsibilities.

Nevertheless, many go on to higher education and the process

5. Patten, Brian quoted by Michael Saward in *And So To Bed?* (Good Reading Ltd., 1975) p. 31

of late adolescence is more drawn out. Amongst such are those still groping for a sense of identity, still battling with unresolved conflicts or still feeling deeply tied to home.

Somehow or other most of us eventually reach adulthood where we can begin to attain our potential as whole persons with a capacity to love, and be loved. Ideally such a young person will be entering a new 'eye-level' adult relationship with his or her parents. More consideration of this growth in maturity will be given in Chapter Three.

CARING FOR ADOLESCENTS

How can we help our adolescent friends towards maturity and a realistic sense of identity?

FAMILY

(a) It is no help to those of us who have adolescent children to be told that our influence on them probably began before they were conceived, whether we have adopted them or not! This daunting thought which points to the quality of relationship between husband and wife will be looked at in Chapters Four and Five when we consider marital counselling.

Nevertheless, we cannot escape completely at this stage as it is clearly established that the *first five to six years of a child's life* are specially important for their emotional and psychological development throughout adolescence. Whether we like it or not, we parents are 'models' or examples of what being 'a father, husband and man' or 'a mother, wife and woman' are about for our children as they grow up through adolescence to adulthood.

ADULTHOOD

ADOLESCENCE

For example, a father who looks to another woman for his sexual interest, should not be surprised to find that his son does the same when he marries (see above, p. 41).

One of the 'problem families' of the Bible was that of Isaac and Rebekah. We read:

> Isaac loved Esau, because he ate of his game; but Rebekah loved Jacob. (Genesis 25:28 RSV)

Esau, hairy and rugged, was a man of action or a man's man, as we might say. Jacob was a 'smoothie' and a home-lover; he was a lady's man and a deceiver. The parents had their favourites and so rivalry, hatred and contemplated murder were the outcomes.

It is interesting to see that Jacob, modelled by his parents' favouritism, was in turn a father who is described as loving his son Joseph more than any other of his children! This Joseph narrowly escaped death at the hands of his enraged brothers.

We should also point to the way that God moulded these men and women of old in spite of themselves. After all, favouritism is only one way of mishandling our children!

More generally, if there is a lack of loving and caring the child *is aware*, is emotionally deprived and will have real difficulties with relationships in adolescence and perhaps beyond. I remember a young man in his twenties who had been adopted. Because he was a quiet and sensitive person, instead of an active sport-loving young man, his mother rejected him. His mother's message to him was, "You're not ours, so we're *not* responsible for the way you are." In many ways he was driven to homosexuality.

(b) Parents need to be *sensitive* to the physical and emotional changes that are taking place so quickly in their adolescent offspring. Clumsy handling can lead to restlessness and insecurity.

Matters of the size of a daughter's breasts or the size of a son's penis are delicate issues to the owners! We need to be specially wary of any teasing if there is late physical development. My sister found it wise to buy bras for both her developing daughters at the same time although the older was less endowed than the younger at that stage.

(c) We must respect the need of adolescents to get away from us and the design and flimsiness of many modern houses are a problem here. A sociological study has shown that children's quarrels are intensified and prolonged by adult interference, and so the old maxim, 'Children should be seen and not heard', could be restated, 'Children should be heard and not seen'. We might add that, in this sense at any rate, "Adolescents should be neither seen nor heard!"

(d) The subject of *discipline* is a vast one. We commonly make two mistakes:

We may be too *authoritarian*, which is the 'big stick' approach of "Do this because I say so". This sort of family is centred on the parents and in Christian circles the impression may be given that "God is on father's side". The children of these families are either mealy-mouthed conformists or raving rebels!

We may be too *permissive*, which is the 'no stick' approach of the child-centred family. Here the parents behave simply as older friends of the child or adolescent. In this sort of family the child is often put on a pedestal and this idealising and idolising may continue into the offspring's adolescence, so that there is a continuing over-dependence on 'dear old Mum and Dad'.

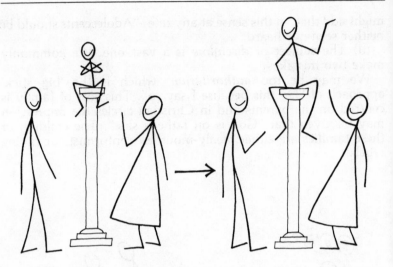

The Christian family should be marked by *Authority with Love* where children obey their parents in the Lord and honour their fathers and mothers, and in turn parents do not provoke their children to anger, bringing them up in the discipline and instruction of the Lord. (Ephesians 6:1-4)

Here there is love, consideration and fairness and a lack of sarcasm, browbeating and nagging.

FRIENDS

Our involvement may be as friends: friends of the family, friends of the needy adolescent, as workers in a caring service for young people, or as school counsellor. Young people desperately need adults who are *good friends* to them. As they move towards adulthood, it is important to see how adults, other than their own parents, handle life. In counselling adolescents we should remember the principles set out in Chapter One, i.e. *involvement, responsibility,* and *right and wrong.* With these in mind, readers may look at the Discussion (p. 49f.) and consider the situation of fifteen-year-old Mavis.

DEATH AND SEPARATION

One key area in adolescent life that we might be called upon to help with as either friend or counsellor is that of death and separation. Here we consider parental death, although the separation and divorce of parents and the death of close friends also have adverse effects.

Death is a taboo subject these days; yet we seem more able to accept the process of mourning in adults than in adolescents. A teenager's ability to come to terms with the death of a parent depends a great deal on the young person's age at the time.

Child up to five or six years. If a parent dies when the child is young there may be considerable difficulty in adolescence.

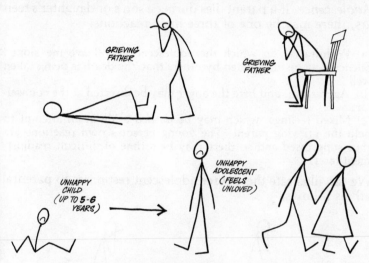

The emotional damage is specially great if the mother dies and there is no mother-substitute (aunt, big sister, etc.).

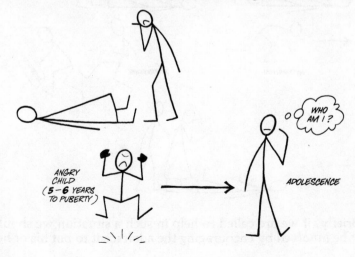

Child five or six years to puberty. During these years, the bereaved child may feel deserted and may well react with anger towards both the dead and the surviving parent (p. 43). At this stage the father has become more important than he was earlier and if he dies his son may have difficulties in adolescence in achieving a sense of being himself. Similarly, his daughter may find it hard to value herself as a woman later.

Adolescence. If a parent dies during a son's or daughter's teen years, there may be one of three main reactions:

(a) Withdrawal, in which the adolescent says 'leave me alone'. Silence may be interpreted by others that 'the death is being taken well'.
(b) Aggression, and here the anger may be directed at the counsellor.
(c) Mixed feelings, which may be pushed aside in an attempt to help the grieving parent. The young person's own reactions are thus suppressed and so there may be a time of difficult readjustment later.

We can illustrate these three adolescent responses to parental death as follows:

WITHDRAWAL

OR
AGGRESSION

COUNSELLOR

OR
SUPPORT

Briefly, if we are called to help in such a situation we should first be *involved* by encouraging the adolescent to put his or her feelings into words. It will be good if the tears can flow as the young person shares the experience and learns to understand it.

Further, we should encourage *responsibility* whereby the grieving adolescent can use their environment to assist mourning. This response is clearest in the girl who has lost her mother and can thereby become the helping mother-substitute for the rest of the family.

However, it is important to sound a word of caution here. In some families, at least in the emotional sense, the bereaved daughter may become a wife-substitute too. Similarly, when a teenage son loses his father he may, lured by the glamour of responsibility, become a husband-substitute for his stricken mother. In both instances, this misplaced sense of commitment may trap the maturing young person into a protracted mutual dependence with the remaining parent. The unfortunate situation may only be relieved by the second marriage of the parent or by a painful bid for freedom by the young person.

There is no doubt that we all need a father-figure and a mother-figure all through life. For many, this emotional and psychological need is met largely by one's earthly parents, especially in those years leading up to and including adolescence. Of course, the adequacy of parents in this respect varies enormously, and the search for mother- and father-substitutes may need to begin early in life. For some, deficient relationships with natural parents can lead to considerable difficulties in believing in and commitment to a loving, Heavenly Father. Yet others, in spite of such disadvantages, find comfort and strength in One who is likened to the very best of fathers (Psalm 103:13, Luke 15:20), yet is also described as having the more motherly attributes of gentleness and tender compassion (Psalm 148:8).

SCHOOL

Though Shakespeare's 'whining school-boy . . . creeping like snail, unwillingly to school' did not *seem* to be, it is important that the early and mid-adolescent should *feel* secure at school as well as at home. Part of this security rests in school and home being *separate* places. Parents should not be 'breathing down teachers' necks' and making endless appointments with the head over every trivial issue. On the other hand, there should be good communication between home and school and both parties should feel that the other is concerned.

It needs to be recognised that during puberty, with its bewildering bodily changes, concentration at study can be less effective. Although this is the age at which abstract thinking begins, it is not the ideal time for pressing adolescents for far-reaching decisions about changes in their syllabuses and future careers.

Mid-adolescents need three to four years of stable relationships with adults to help with their sense of identity and thus good, secure relationships with their teachers are very important. This is a more realistic age for choices about the future although one still sees students at University who look back at mistaken decisions about subjects taken.

CONCLUSION

As in the first chapter, we have seen the way that the Fall of man affects all of us, so that parents repeat unbalanced patterns learnt from their parents and so pass these on to their children. We have been reminded how such imbalance may be aggravated by authoritarian or permissive parents. We have seen that adult friends may play a crucial part in redressing the balance.

We should see that in Christ the Generation Gap can be narrowed and even obliterated. There is a suggestion of this in Malachi 4:6 where we read, 'that he will turn the hearts of fathers to their children and the hearts of children to their fathers . . .'

We can remember that the only glimpse we have of Christ in early adolescence shows both his obedience to his earthly parents and his awareness of the higher authority of his heavenly Father (Luke 2:49-52).

Our roles as parents and as friends of young people should include helping them to take heed of the words in Ecclesiastes 12:1 before adulthood comes with its possibility of cynicism:

'Remember also your Creator in the days of your youth, before the evil days come, and the years draw nigh, when you will say, "I have no pleasure in them".'

FOR FURTHER READING

Cousins, P. *Christianity and Sexual Literation* (Exeter, The Paternoster Press) 1972

Hollings, M. and Gullick, E. *You Must be Joking, Lord* (London, Mayhew McCrimmon) 1975

Laufer, M. *Adolescent Disturbance and Breakdown* (London, Penguin Books) 1975

Leech, K. *Youthquake* (London, The Sheldon Press) 1973

Miller, D. *The Age Between* (London, Cornmarket/Hutchinson) 1969

FOR DISCUSSION

You have been friendly with the Joneses since they moved into your locality one year ago, from the other side of the country.

Mr. Jones is quiet, shy and does not communicate easily. He works at a bank and is away most weekends visiting a sick mother a few hundred miles away.

Mrs. Jones is a great doer and some say that she 'wears the trousers'. She had an unhappy childhood and was rather starved of love. She serves huge meals and is very bothered if the children spurn the large helpings she gives. She is herself overweight.

There are three children: Mavis (15), John (11), and Jane (8). John and Jane are well behaved and 'never put a foot wrong'. Mavis is different.

Mrs. Jones has asked you whether you can 'do anything with Mavis as she has been impossible lately'. She has been both verbally rude and sulky and stays out till midnight after parties, although her mother insists that she is home by 10.30pm. During the last fortnight she has played truant from the local school on two occasions.

You have had a good chat with Mavis and find that behind the tears she seems to be very resentful about something. You learn that she stole a bar of chocolate from the supermarket whilst playing truant, and no-one else knows. She also admits to smoking pot a few times recently and says that she is in love with the Geography teacher, Mr. Mountain.

(1) Do you find yourself taking sides in this situation?

(2) If so, whose?

Mr. Jones's	John and Jane's
Mrs. Jones's	Mr. Mountain's
Grandmother's	The Supermarket's
Mavis's	The Law's

(3) If you take sides, try to put into words your feelings on the situation as if you were the person you identify with.

(4) What are the likely reasons for Mavis's resentment?

Her grandmother's illness?
Her father's remoteness?
Her mother's attempts to control her?
The recent move?
The 'goodness' of her brother and sister?
Any other?

(5) How would you deal with Mavis's law-breaking?

Tell her parents?
Advise Mavis to tell her parents?
Tell the police?
Advise Mavis to tell the police?
Tell her to make amends at the supermarket?
Advise her to tell no-one else?

(6) Would you plan to talk things over with:

Her parents by themselves?
Mrs. Jones alone?
Mrs. Jones and Mavis together?
Mr. Jones alone?
Her parents and Mavis together?

(7) Have you kept in mind the principles of:

Involvement?
Responsibility?
Right and Wrong?

(If you are studying this book in a group, a very good way of handling this material, as well as the situations described at the ends of chapters three and four, would be to act a series of thumb-nail sketches based on the information provided. This will help you to identify better with other people's problems, and may also give you useful insights into yourself and other members of the group. The situations acted can then be discussed in the group, following the questions given above or allowing more free-ranging discussions. Scenes that could be acted might include:

(a) A discussion between Mr. and Mrs. Jones about their three children.

(b) A scene involving Mavis and her brother and sister over some expected duty, for example washing up.

(c) A scene when Mavis, returning at midnight after one of her parties, is confronted by her parents.

(d) A situation where Mavis is talking to a couple of school friends about her various exploits.)

CHAPTER THREE
Being Single

I approach this chapter's subject with some diffidence as I personally have not been single for about fifteen years! Nonetheless, nearly all my patients are single and many of our closest friends are unmarried.

WHY SO LITTLE ABOUT BEING SINGLE?

If you go to a Christian bookshop you will find a great array of books on the privileges and problems of marriage and family life, but very little on friendship and being single. In talking of a third person, it is interesting to observe how often one will say, "Oh, he or she is *just* a friend." The inference can be that marriage and family are all important but friendship and singleness are second rate states! Along the same lines, why is it there are numerous marriage guidance counsellors, but a single life counsellor is a comparatively rare fish?

Why is singleness so little thought of in Church and Society? I would suggest that these three reasons are relevant:

(1) The Bible says comparatively little about the single life. In the Old Testament, marriage was an integral part of the life of God's people with the exception of wandering holy men. Young women would marry as soon as they were able to have children and, furthermore, in the patriarchal period and through into the monarchy, polygamy was frequently practised. For example, at a quick count, David seems to have had at least eight wives! To stay single in those days must have been quite an effort.

In the New Testament we can make a more fruitful study on singleness in the life of Our Lord and the teachings of the unmarried Paul.

(2) The Church has played down the concept of friendship in its history, partly as a reaction to the elevated view of it in the pagan Greek world of Plato and Aristotle. Roman Catholics have been drawn by their teaching towards the virtue of celibacy, whereas the norm of marriage has been strongly emphasised by Protestants. On the one hand, the single life has been

viewed as especially virtuous and spiritual, and on the other, as
too embarrassing a matter to be faced squarely.

(3) Western society has become increasingly obsessed with
sex as the mainspring for all that we think or do. As a result, it
can be very difficult for us to be straightforward about the
friendships of being single. The implication seems to be that all
such relationships must lead to the bedroom sooner or later.
Try convincing someone that your friendship is Platonic, and
you may be met with a snigger or a knowing wink.

Let us try to correct some of the distortion there is in both
Christian and non-Christian thinking about being single.

OUR SEXUALITY

Our first task is to spend a little time reminding ourselves that
we are sexual beings. Most of us, if we are honest, do not need
reminding! Nevertheless, as we think about being single we
must consider the whole person, which includes his or her
sexuality. Incidentally, much of what I write under this heading
applies not only to the man or woman who has not married, but
also to the divorced and widowed. Bereavement in marriage
and marital breakdown will also be considered in the final
chapter.

In Chapter One we considered that God made us in His own
image. Let us now look more closely at Genesis 1:27:

'So God created man in His own image, in the image of God
He created him; male and female He created them.'

Do you notice the progression of thought? 'In the image of
God', 'He created *him*' and then the surprising statement that
tells us so much about the nature of Man, 'male and female He
created *them*'. A Frenchman once said that between man and
woman there is little difference but "Vive la différence!" God
made men and women different — different in appearance and
certain bodily functions, different genetically with different
recipes of hormones in the blood stream, all the differences of
masculinity and femininity, of male and female sexuality.

As we saw in Chapter Two, an essential aspect of adolescence
is developing a sense of masculinity or femininity. This is helped
by wise and loving parents as well as real friends, so that we can
grow up from childhood to adulthood.

As adults, moving towards an increasing maturity, we need to
recognise, be thankful for and commit to Christ's lordship our
sexuality, whether we are single or double. Paul's general claim
in 1 Timothy 4:4, 'For everything created by God is good, and

nothing is to be rejected if it is received with thanksgiving' should fashion our attitudes toward our sexual natures.

One of our main challenges in this chapter will be to face the implications of the God-given sexuality of the single man and woman. This sexuality needs to be understood and used in legitimate and loving ways, whether or not in God's good time it is given its most intimate expression within the commitment of marriage.

OUR BODIES

Before thinking about the sexual aspects of being single more closely, we need to consider in general terms our attitudes towards our bodies.

The Victorians have received a certain notoriety in their prudishness about the body. It is a standard joke that the sight of legs, even table legs, was offensive to the Victorian eyes and mind, and so the table coverings swept down to the floor! The Victorian doctor had special difficulties in reaching his more well-to-do patients in order to examine them. As Brian Craddock has written: 'The number of lacy, calico, poplin, horsehair, dimity, cambric, merino, camlet, alpaca, winsey, linsey, silk, satin, steel and velvet hurdles that had to be negotiated before you got to the patient was astounding.'[1]

Although most of us are less prudish than our Victorian ancestors, many Christians are still trapped by a way of thinking about their bodies that is more Ancient Greek than Christian!

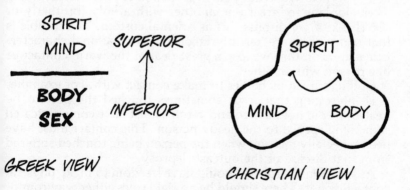

1. Craddock, Brian. Article in *Rostrum*, July 1975 (Pfizer Ltd., 1975)

In contrast to the Christian view of man as a whole being, the pagan Greek view of you and me is that our spirits and minds are superior in every way to our bodies. This pre-Christian double-view or dualism can lead us to a particular imbalance where we rush feverishly from one church meeting to another, neglecting our God-given abilities to think, feel, do and be. Our bodies and minds may thus be neglected and our horizons so limited that we become unfit and deadly boring!

A CHRISTIAN GONE GREEK

Someone has said that it is as though many of us misunderstood the context of when the risen Lord said, "Touch me not". We are afraid to touch one another. We are the 'great untouchables'. When we read Paul's greetings to the Romans and Thessalonians to 'greet one another with a holy (brotherly or sisterly) kiss' we dismiss this as oriental custom. The trouble is that many of us are 'terribly English' and a national characteristic can mean that we lose a great deal of the warm contact of one person with another.

God has given us bodies to make contact with. For example, it is interesting that Jesus sometimes touched the part to be healed; he did not have to and yet this must have communicated something special to the needy person. This contact must have been especially moving when the person being touched suffered from that disease of the outcast, leprosy.

As with Our Lord, we should have freedom to make physical contact or not. There should be no rigid rules either way round. On the one hand we have often erred towards being cold and undemonstrative. On the other hand, the specialness of such

encounters is lost if we are all over one another all the time!
There must be spontaneity and above all sincerity; where such
qualities exist we may gain much from the welcoming hand-
shake, the hand on the shoulder, the kiss of friendship and the
loving embrace.

We need then to capture a much wider view of our sexuality.
We tend to narrow this word down simply to the matter of
sexual intercourse. This is of course something very special and
as Christians, we should understand that this is an expression of
committed love designed for marriage. However, a true understanding of ourselves will help us to see that facial expressions,
gestures, movements, ways of thinking, words and actions can
all be coloured by our sexuality as men and women made in
God's image.

COPING WITH THE SEXUAL URGE

It is one thing to express ourselves through our bodies more
warmly and generously as we have just considered; it is another
thing to cope with and harness strong sexual desires. Michel
Quoist in his *Prayers of Life* dedicates a prayer *To Love* and,
although it is further entitled *The Prayer of an Adolescent*, it is
a prayer than any lonely person could echo:

> I want to love, Lord.
> I need to love.
> All my being is desire;
> My heart,
> My body,
>   yearn in the night towards an unknown one to love.
> My arms thrash about and I can seize on no object for my love.
> I am alone and want to be two.
> I speak, and no one is there to listen.
> I live, and no one is there to share my life.
> Why be so rich and have no one to enrich?
> Where does this love come from?
> Where is it going?
> I want to love, Lord,
> I need to love.
> Here this evening, Lord, is all my love, unused.[2]

We have thought a little about the positive use of our bodies
and emotions in Christian fellowship. We would add to this the
whole concept of loving service to others and we will look at the
value of friendship later in the chapter. However, for the

2. Quoist, Michel. *Prayers of Life* (Logos Books, 1963) p. 38

moment we need to consider the more negative aspect of 'coping with the urge', i.e. self control.

Masturbation

This was mentioned briefly in the last chapter as we thought about early adolescence. We saw then that masturbation is not in itself wrong, but it is a pale shadow of real love-making. It may be helpful to consider a few further points on this wide-spread habit.

I would like to recommend Margaret Evening's book *Who Walk Alone* for her wise treatment of this subject and many other aspects of being single.[3] She helpfully distinguishes two types of masturbation. First, she writes of 'that which is explosive and urgent, that gives immediate physical relief to a sudden immense build-up of sexual energy'. She pleads here for a sense of proportion and says, 'The best way to overcome it is to play down the importance of it'.

Secondly, she describes a masturbation which is 'a self-indulgent luxury, a deliberate turning away from reality, a way of stimulating or supporting sexual fantasies'. In times of isola-tion and loneliness, masturbation may be a means of seeking solace and a sense of well-being. In situations like this, Christians may find a special help in an awareness of God's loving nearness.

Margaret Evening rightly adds that this is a 'battle of the mind' and one must be essentially practical in doing battle. *Not* necessarily, as one camp leader suggested, "going to bed wearing boxing gloves"! Some will find it helps to keep active by planning the next day, writing letters, etc. until one is tired enough to get to sleep quickly. Others will find a good bed-time book (careful choice is needed here!) or the slow careful meditation on a psalm is helpful last thing.

Remember, the habit is widespread; so much so that one man went to a counsellor in distress because he feared he was abnormal. He had never masturbated!

Lust

Here again we must seek a balance. Our Lord said, "I say to you that every one who looks at a woman lustfully has already committed adultery with her in his heart." The idea behind the word translated as 'lustfully' here is the entertaining of a strong wish that a certain forbidden thing might happen, in this case,

3. Evening, Margaret. *Who Walk Alone* (Hodder & Stoughton, 1974) p. 30-36

sexual intercourse with an attractive woman to whom one is not committed in marriage. This is nothing to do with feeling our pulse race when someone with a devastating figure crosses our field of vision!

The Hot Situation

The story of Joseph in Potiphar's household includes a 'hot situation' involving a married woman and a single young man. Potiphar's wife was well-off and had too little to do; she was probably bored and possibly sexually frustrated in that her husband may have been an eunuch. Into her affluent, easy-going life came Joseph, 'handsome and good looking'. After a time she sat up and took notice and, we read in Genesis 39, 'cast her eyes on Joseph and said, "Lie with me" '. (The Bible is so simple; a modern novel would take a whole chapter to lead up to such a situation!) She persisted day after day, hot with desire. One day, alone in the house together, she grabbed his garment urging, "Lie with me". He twisted and shook free, leaving the tell-tale garment. We can tell she felt *lust* for Joseph rather than love, because he is falsely accused of rape, and imprisoned.

It is instructive to see how Joseph handled the situation: "How then can I do this great wickedness, and sin against God?" He saw that his first loyalty was to God, the God who made sex good and special.

Homosexuality

This is an important subject in its own right and, unfortunately, we must be brief in a book of this size.

Although homosexuality is very much 'on the map' today, it has been around a long time; it is said that fourteen out of the first fifteen Roman Emperors were homosexual. Today, thinking on homosexuality is often expressed in words like these, "We think that being gay is one of the most positive aspects of our lives."

What do we mean by homosexuality? We can define a homosexual as a man or woman with *habitual* feelings of sexual attraction towards others of the same sex. If the sexual feelings for the opposite sex are still slight or even absent when adulthood is reached, then the term 'invert' is sometimes used. If homosexual practice is indulged in for 'kicks' or for different sexual experience, then the word 'pervert' may be used for the person so behaving. Such pejorative labels as 'invert' and 'pervert' are best avoided.

From the Bible we can make two main points about homosexuality. First, being homosexual is not part of God's original plan. God made woman to be man's sexual partner, not another man and, for that matter, not the beasts. Secondly, sexual intercourse with the same sex as a perversion is clearly condemned, e.g. 'Remember Sodom and Gomorrah, they committed fornication and followed *unnatural lusts;* and they paid the penalty in eternal fire, an example for all to see' (Jude 7).

From this, we should see that God does *not* condemn anyone for simply being homosexual and neither should we. I wonder how many church fellowships have the same welcome towards someone who bravely admits that he or she is homosexual, as they do to others? In our Christian caring we should seek to understand the problems of the homosexual who often feels isolated and condemned by others. I would specially recommend Alex Davidson's book *The Returns of Love* for a sympathetic insight into homosexuality. It is written as a series of letters between two Christian homosexual men, and as such highlights the heartache and heart-searching of their dilemma. A sense of isolation is brought out in this passage:

"With me, these introspective moods of self-pity are the result not so much of depression as of loneliness. Those two don't necessarily go together, for it may be on a day when I haven't a care in the world that the consciousness of my solitude descends on me out of a clear sky, and tempts me to imagine, and even to seek, liaisons which are imprudent or exclusive or just plain immoral — whatever is on hand to meet the suddenly-realised need. A tremendous help then is a wide circle of healthy friendships, and I'm grateful for those which have been given to me."[4]

These diagrams illustrate in an oversimplified way certain factors which can contribute to the development of homosexuality in the adult person:

4. Davidson, Alex. *The Returns of Love* (IVP, 1970) p. 54-55

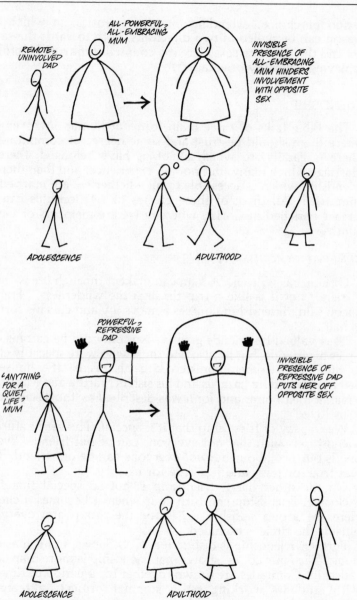

We need to be careful in concluding that a person is essentially homosexual. As we saw in Chapter Two, sexual identity can be problematic to the adolescent. There is often a prolonged period of choice, extending into the twenties, in which the person can be pulled in two directions, both towards the same sex and the opposite sex. Here the counsellor may be helpful in achieving a healthy orientation.

FRIENDSHIP

The Bible talks of three main forms of human involvement where there should be trust and some degree of commitment. There is Family, to which all of us have belonged; there is Marriage which many, but not all, experience; and then there is Friendship which is accessible to all whether we are married or unmarried. All three of these groups of relationships can be further enriched in Christ, whereby we are members of God's family.

GENERAL CONSIDERATIONS

Olthuis has written, 'A man can make it through life without a friend, but it is like a trip through the wilderness.'[5] Francis Bacon said, 'Friendship doubles a man's joy and cuts his sorrow in half'.

Jesus valued his friends greatly. Not only did he call his disciples his friends, but he also had those who were specially close to him. The women ministered to his needs; the house at Bethany shared by Lazarus and his sisters Martha and Mary was a real home to him; and John was described as 'the disciple that Jesus loved'.

We can say of friendship that it is *special*. The very nature of friendship is such that not everyone can be our friends. Everyone is our neighbour but *not* everyone can be our friend. This was true for Jesus and it is true for us.

On the other hand, friendship is not so special that it is exclusive. Friendship can turn sour when it becomes a clique. Here the group selfishly exists for the group and everyone outside the circle is excluded.

Further, friendship is *distinctive*. C. S. Lewis, in his masterly book, *The Four Loves*, shows that friendship is more than comradeship. Comrades are drawn together for a period of time, as with students working on a summer project, a team of Christians helping with a Mission, a supporters' club shouting for their favourite football team, or a group of actors working

5. Olthuis, James H. *I Pledge You My Troth* (Harper & Row, 1975) p. 110

on a play. Obviously any of these comrades may also become friends.

C. S. Lewis says that the typical expression of an opening friendship is, "What? You too? I thought I was the only one."[6] At the age of eleven I met the boy who later married my sister; we became firm friends all those years ago when we discovered that we both got excited at the thought of spotted flycatchers nesting in the guttering of his parents' house! It was this common interest that drew us together and friendship began.

C. S. Lewis further distinguishes friends from lovers: 'We picture lovers face to face but friends side by side, their eyes look ahead'.[7]

We can summarise the distinctiveness of friendship as follows:

FRIENDS....

NOT COMRADES

NOT LOVERS

QUALITIES OF FRIENDS

We might pick out four of the more important qualities of friendship which the Bible describes. Friends should be:

Constant

Here there are qualities of trust and commitment. Not that it is fashionable for us to make the sort of life-long vows that David and Jonathan made. In fact, we may feel that something is lost when friendship is talked about.

Proverbs sees this quality of friendship as sometimes more binding even that blood ties; e.g. Proverbs 18:24. "There are friends who pretend to be friends, but there is a friend who sticks closer than a brother." As we saw in the last chapter, there is a great need for such friendships that bridge the so-called 'generation gap' — Proverbs 27:10 points this out, "Your friend, and your father's friend, do not forsake; and do not go

6. Lewis, C. S. *The Four Loves* (Fontana, 1963) p. 62
7. Lewis, C. S. op. cit. p. 63

to your brother's house in the day of your calamity". Here we can see the importance of the adult 'friend of the family' to both generations.

Honest

Proverbs speaks of true friendship, where wounding words may be spoken in love, as in chapter 27:6, 'Faithful are the wounds of a friend; profuse are the kisses of an enemy'. This loving honesty is contrasted with the insincere praise of more shallow relationships, spoken of in Proverbs 29:5, 'A man who flatters his neighbour spreads a net for his feet'.

Sharing

Jesus made this very clear when He said to His disciples, "I have called you friends, for all that I have heard from my Father I have made known to you" (John 15:5).

Sharing between friends should include the healthy clash of views and personalities. This is suggested by Proverbs 27:17 where we read, 'Iron sharpens iron and one man sharpens another'.

Tactful

True friendship is sensitive and is marked by a respect for another's feelings. A lack of friendship is indicated where, for example, a person is hearty at the wrong time! This sort of insensitivity is seen in Proverbs 27:14, 'He who blesses his neighbour with a loud voice rising early in the morning will be counted as cursing'. Those who share accommodation know how friendship can be strained to breaking point by such untimely exuberance!

Another example of a lack of tact in friendship is not knowing when a joke has gone too far. Proverbs 26:18, 19 puts this graphically: 'Like a madman who throws firebrands, arrows and death, is the man who deceives his neighbour and says, "I am only joking!" '

TYPES OF FRIENDSHIP

Having established a few of the essential qualities that true friends should have, let us now consider the single person in his or her friendships under three main headings:

Same Sex Friendships

One of the best known classical friendships of a deeply committed nature was that of the two young men, David and Jonathan. Although their relationship was strengthened by a common adversary, the unpredictable King Saul, there is no doubt that there was an intense and enduring mutual attraction between them. We read this of their first encounter: 'The soul of Jonathan was knit to the soul of David, and Jonathan loved him as his own soul' (1 Samuel 18:1). Years later, when David lamented the death of Saul and Jonathan killed in battle, he cried, "I am distressed for you, my brother Jonathan; very pleasant have you been to me; your love to me was wonderful, passing the love of women" (2 Samuel 1:26 RSV). (This last remark was quite a comment for the amorous David!)

Some have implied that here was a homosexual love affair, but this seems to me to be extremely unlikely in the face of the forbidden nature of such an alliance, bearing in mind the commitment of these two young men unashamedly before their God. Further, such a smear as that seems to imply that there can be no strong relationship between two men or two women without homosexuality or lesbianism being the heart of the matter. C. S. Lewis pricks the balloon of this sort of false accusation in his *The Four Loves*:

'The fact that no positive evidence of homosexuality can be discovered in the behaviour of two Friends does not disconcert the wiseacres at all; "That", they say gravely, "is just what we should expect." The very lack of evidence is thus treated as evidence; the absence of smoke proves that the fire is very carefully hidden. Yes — if it exists at all. But we must first prove its existence. Otherwise we are arguing like a man who should say, "If there were an invisible cat in that chair, the chair would look empty; but the chair does look empty; therefore there is an invisible cat in it".'[8]

There is a Chinese proverb which says, 'It is better to travel and not to arrive than not to have travelled at all'; and I suspect that David and Jonathan and countless others since, for whom special friendships have been of great importance, would have agreed. Archbishop Lang, for example, once said that in the loneliness of his bachelor life his great need was not for friends, of whom he had plenty, any more than it was for work, of which he had too much. It was for that old, simple, human thing — someone in daily nearness to love.

Yet there is a danger for a *special* friendship between two men or two women to become an *exclusive* friendship. How can this

8. Lewis, C. S. op. cit. p. 58

be prevented? Margaret Evening in _Who Walk Alone_[9] suggests a few guidelines which I have illustrated. She argues that friendship should not be so special that any other friend is neglected or considered a nuisance:

Further, friendship should not be so special that jealousy creeps in:

The jealousy illustrated may, of course, work in the opposite direction in which the favourite friend is jealous of any potential rival and works hard to ward off any intrusion.

Thirdly, friendship should not be so special that it affects normal relationships with the opposite sex:

Opposite Sex Friendships

Here we are considering a relationship between a single man and a single woman in which they are friends and not lovers. Obviously such a situation may lead from friendship into erotic love and in the next chapter we will think together about relationships of such loving, where marriage may be the outcome.

First of all, let us think about a few of the _dangers_ of such

9. Evening, Margaret. op. cit. p. 46-47

friendships before we look at them more positively. The first of these is *one-sidedness*. Sadly, and commonly, one of the two friends may become more deeply involved than the other. (See the illustration below). The degrees of expectation may differ sharply. He may be deeply contented with their concert-going and long discussions, and she may develop 'ringing in the ears'(A). The danger is, that fearing to lose him, she may say nothing of how she feels and from her point of view the friendship may become more and more exclusive (B). Although difficult, it is surely wiser to be honest for both of their sakes. This may mean the end of their friendship (C) or they may be able to continue their friendship on a different basis with a better understanding (D).

FIG A

FIG B

The second danger to consider is *imbalance*. As we have seen in Chapters One and Two, we may develop emotionally in a lopsided way and this may spoil the quality of friendships between men and women.

For example, a rather passive young man, with a background of spoiling and being 'mum's little boy', may well meet and enjoy being engulfed by a mothering, smothering sort of young woman!

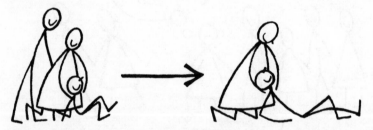

Alternatively, a woman with a sheltered background may lure her man by playing the defenceless female. He may enjoy being the big, strong provider, but they may well be trapped into a possessive and joyless existence:

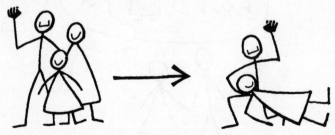

Such imbalance in friendship may greatly delay growth in maturity for both parties.

In spite of these two dangers, the joys and privileges of more mature friendship between the sexes are many. We have mentioned how important such relationships were to Jesus. There is no doubt that we too could be greatly enriched by friendships in which there is a much greater *openness* than we are accustomed to. Men need the tenderness and trust of women; women need the honour, respect and warmth of acceptance that men can give.

It would be very healthy to see a coming together of men and women in friendship, to serve and create in the body of Christ. Here the complementarity of qualities that we may regard as more masculine, such as organisational ability and objective thinking, and those we think of as more feminine, such as perception and practical common-sense, could be used gloriously for the Lord and for one another.

Friendships with Married Couples

For many, this is the most controversial area of all with the perennial fear of the triangular relationship of husband, wife and another man or woman. The Bible says that 'God sets the solitary (or the lonely) in families' (Psalm 68:6). Then why are there so many lonely, single people who are *not* 'set in families'?

There are many reasons, but I believe that an important one is that many families are afraid, because of their own insecurity or selfishness, to take loving risks with their single friends. Let us look at this more closely, considering two of the problems, as well as the pleasures of such relationships.

The first problem is that of the *'boltless door'*. Where married people are happy to open their home in this way, it is easy for both sides of the friendship to forget that the door has a bolt or a lock on the inside. Proverbs warns of this situation in 25:17, 'Let your foot be seldom in your neighbour's house, lest he become weary of you and hate you'.

The fault may be with the married friends. They have said, "Millicent, you *know* that you are welcome *any* time, *always.*" And they meant it! Perhaps Millicent cannot be blamed for believing them in her loneliness. They are nearby; they have a colour television; the children adore Millicent, and so does the cat. It may not be many months before there is an established bush telegraph that Millicent is on her way yet again, and the family flies for the weekend in the car!

Again, there is the need for honesty in such a friendship, and a greater sensitivity of mutual needs can still be developed.

The second problem is that of the *'eternal triangle'*. Although, where a marriage is stable, there is little threat of a love relationship developing between a husband and a single woman friend or a wife and a single man friend, it is important to realise that it can happen to anyone! This is one of the risks of such friendship, and with God's grace the development is preventable. Again, if friendship is changing to love, a way through can be found where there is honesty and a determination to save the marriage.

Margaret Evening writes of a friend who loved deeply a married man with whom she worked. His wife was well aware of this mutual admiration and respect between the single friend and her husband, but she was secure in herself and did not feel excluded. Another secret of this situation was the three-fold nature of the friendship; the man's wife and the single woman were also firm friends who shared a great deal.[10]

This diagram illustrates the uniqueness and priority of the marriage bond, together with a mutual friendship with a single person. The risks have just been considered, but in spite of these there can be enrichment for all three people:

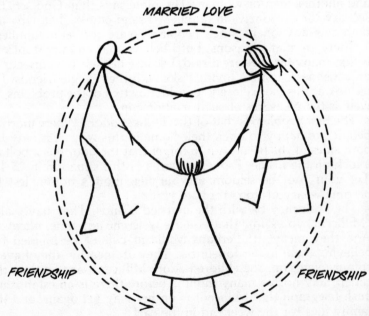

MARRIED LOVE

FRIENDSHIP   FRIENDSHIP

In all this, it is essential to know the difference between marriage and friendship. Olthuis has written this about such a triangular situation: 'The myth that all close contact necessarily

10. Evening, Margaret, op. cit. p. 101

leads to physical intercourse is just that — a myth. We must free ourselves from its deadening influence. Friendship is a God-given way to be intimate which does not involve physical inter-course. Of course, casual physical contact does play a role in friendship. But such physical contact always retains its limited role.'[11]

FELLOWSHIP

It is important to place all that we have said about friendship, including our sexuality, under the Lordship of Christ in the fellowship of his church. To see this in context we might say that everyone is our neighbour, many are our brothers and sisters in Christ, and a few are our friends.

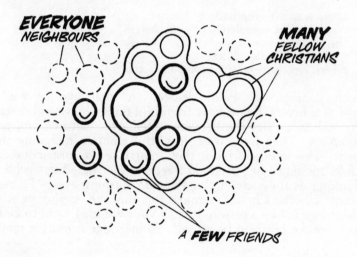

CONCLUSION

What is the way forward for the single person whom we are trying to help? Is it to be frustration or fulfilment?

FRUSTRATION?

There are at least two quite common attitudes to being single which can so easily lead to frustration. The first is 'poor little me'. Such thoughts of self-pity may create greater problems for women, who often have a deep-seated need for security, per-manence, home-making and having children. An unpublished

11. Olthuis, James H. op. cit. p. 115

survey amongst Christian women in the late 1960s revealed nearly 70% as unhappy about being single at some stage in their adult lives, with a peak in the early 30's.[12] Men, too, can feel left on the shelf', and can be tempted to 'poor little me' in their late 20's, 30's or 40's. All their contemporaries seem to have found ideal, beautiful wives and apparently are living in wedded bliss!

In 'poor little me', it is as if one says, "Unless *I* do something about it *and* quickly, I shall *never* be able to get married. I can't rely on God here; it's too close to the heart; it's too 'me'. He'll never turn anyone up, so *I'm* on the warpath!"

The second way to frustration is the approach, 'I'll never marry!' Some single men and women can be rather like the young lady of Lucca:

> There was a Young Lady of Lucca
> Whose lovers completely forsook her;
> She ran up a tree
> And said, "Fiddle-de-dee!"
> Which embarrassed the people of Lucca.

Such people say "Fiddle-de-dee!" to marriage as well as potential lovers. Some good friends of ours who would describe themselves as 'free-thinkers' are intelligent, cultured and good company. They have four delightful children including three girls. The mother feels that marriage is restrictive and undermining to her personal freedom. Her daughters echo her thinking as they say smilingly, with flashing eyes, "I'll never marry". Some Christians make this mistake, saying in effect, "Marriage is like a prison; it clips your wings. I want to be free to serve the Lord, to be myself. So marriage is *not* for me!"

FULFILMENT?

Are there more constructive attitudes towards being single? The scriptures seem to indicate at least two basic principles to help unmarried people towards fulfilment. First of all, *God has a plan*. This can be difficult to believe when it is hard to find interesting friends of the opposite sex, or when one promising relationship after another breaks down. There is no doubt that both Jesus and Paul said that *some* are called to a single life and should see this in terms of a gift from God (Matthew 19:12; 1 Corinthians 7:7). Many, however, have no such clear mandate and need to see the way forward in terms of an openness

12. Welch, Margaret. *Private Communication*, March, 1975

towards God's 'good, acceptable and perfect will' (Romans 12:2). Whether we eventually marry or not and if we allow Him to, God will see us *all the way* through life. As he says in Isaiah 46 3f., 'A load on me from your birth, carried by me from the womb; till you grow old I am He, and when white hairs come, I will carry you still; I have made you and I will bear the burden, I will carry you and bring you to safety.'

Secondly, we should *be positive about being single.* In our emphasis on friendship in this chapter, we have tried to be just that. Paul, who has been much misunderstood in this area, was of course single like Our Lord and he said some very positive things about the unmarried state in 1 Corinthians 7. Much of this, he explained, was his own, personal view and should be understood in the light of the urgency of the times. His main point is that to be single means that we can also be *single-minded* in serving the Lord with an undivided attention for the job in hand. It means, too, that there are greater opportunities for relaxation, for the following of interests and the forging of friendships than most married people have, at least short of retirement! Gini Andrews has written, 'Some of the most interesting people I know are single. Often they have developed their minds and skills in a way married people have not had time to do . . .'[13]

Finally, in trying to help our single friends in need, we do well if we can encourage them to accept their sexuality and channel it aright, if we can help them to value friendship in all its rich variety, and if they, for their part, can trust God for the future with an openness towards him, rejoicing in the difficulties and privileges of being single.

FOR FURTHER READING

Andrews, G. *Your Half of the Apple* (London, Marshall, Morgan & Scott) 1972
Davidson, A. *The Returns of Love* (Leicester, IVP) 1970
Evening, M. *Who Walk Alone* (London, Hodder & Stoughton) 1974
Moss, R. *Christians and Homosexuality* (Exeter, The Paternoster Press) 1977
West, D. J. *Homosexuality* (London, Penguin Books Ltd.) 1969

13. Andrews, Gini. *Your Half of the Apple* (Lakeland, 1972) p. 155

FOR DISCUSSION

Monica, aged thirty and unmarried, has 'phoned you and told you that she would like to talk over a few things with you. She lives with two other young women in a flat and has a reasonably well paid secretarial job. Her father whom she loved greatly died when she was fifteen. Her mother remarried three years later. Although she is fond of her mother, she has always rather resented the remarriage and is cool about her stepfather.

She tells you that she feels increasingly unhappy although she cannot say why. She has had no regular boyfriend since her early twenties. He reminded her of her father but she was shattered to discover after six months that he was already married, had been separated but was now returning to his wife. Since then, she has felt remote from other people with the exception of one of her flat-mates, Ermentrude.

Ermentrude is a warm, motherly figure of the same age and seems to enjoy picking Monica up when she is down. Monica has found herself wanting to be with her more and more and they have planned a holiday in the Lake District together. She has also recently been told that Ermentrude plans to visit the USA for a year to join her family.

The third flat dweller is Gloria who is very attractive and has a constant stream of male admirers. Monica hates her. One of Gloria's ex-boyfriends, Augustus, has asked Monica out.

(1) Why is Monica unhappy?

Because her father died fifteen years ago?
Because her mother remarried?
Because she was deceived by her boyfriend?
Because she virtually has no friends?
Because she fears she is too involved with Ermentrude?
Because Ermentrude is leaving?
Because she shares a flat with Gloria?
Because Augustus has asked her out?

(2) What is your aim in helping her?

To help her overcome resentment and hatred?
To encourage Ermentrude and Monica to settle down together?
To find new friends?
To 'marry her off'?
For her to attend your local church?

(As with the other suggestions for discussion, it may be helpful to act one or two scenes from this situation. Apart from being fun to do, this experience should help the group in its understanding of the problems involved. A scene that might be usefully explored is one in which the motherly Ermentrude, the depressed Monica and the glamorous Gloria are preparing a meal to which an unknown number of Gloria's admirers has been invited; Augustus arrives unexpectedly early at the height of the three women's interaction.

Another way of using this material would be for two members of the group to act as Monica and the Counsellor. The rest of the group can observe this interchange then add their comments in discussion following.)

CHAPTER FOUR

Marital Counselling — Early Years

In Chapter One we considered three principles of Christian caring: Involvement, Responsibility, and Right and Wrong. In the
next two chapters we looked at Adolescence and then Being
Single and tried to apply these principles in various situations.
In the last two chapters we have the daunting task of considering how to help our married friends who are in difficulty.

In this chapter we will think about the biblical foundations of
marriage, their practical outworking for living as husband and
wife and the matter of counselling married people in need, with
a special emphasis on the early years of marriage. To tackle this,
we need first to turn our gaze on to the single person as we did
in Chapter Three. There, the emphasis was on friendship,
known to the Greeks as *philia;* now we must start by thinking
about 'being in love', a form of love to which the Greeks gave
the name *eros.*

BEING IN LOVE?

In the last chapter, we left our two single people holding hands
and resolutely looking ahead, sharing their common interests.
Now they are in love!

What do we mean by 'being in love'? Poets, authors and
writers of dictionaries have been trying to define this since
ancient times. Simply because we are human beings, most of us
have some idea deep in our bones what 'being in love' means.
C. S. Lewis in *The Four Loves* makes some helpful points. He
says that if you ask a man who is in love what he wants, the true
reply will often be, "to go on thinking of her". He says that we
must not confuse 'being in love' with sexual desire, although to
be in love is bound to include a measure of sexual longing
sooner or later. "Sexual desire," C. S. Lewis says, "without Eros
(i.e. 'being in love') wants *it*, the *thing* in itself. Eros wants the
Beloved."[1]

The Song of Songs in the Old Testament gives a beautifully
poetic description of what it is like to be in love and the point

1. Lewis, C. S. *The Four Loves* (Fontana Books, 1963) p. 87

just made is brought out in, for example, Song of Songs 7:10, 'I am my beloved's and his desire is for me'. Notice that it says 'for me' and not 'for it'. We could amplify this as, 'his desire is for me as a whole person and not simply for my body'. This desire for the loved one is hinted at when lovers playfully say to each other, "I could eat you!"

Walter Trobisch underlines the complexity of being in love in his booklet *Here is my Problem*. 'Love is a feeling to be learned. It is tension and fulfilment; it is deep longing and hostility; it is gladness and it is pain. There is not one without the other.'

This then is the delightful but often agonizing state that our two friends are now in. Inevitably, there are two common tendencies which people in love can be trapped by and these mistaken ways of being can prevent the maturing of love between a man and a woman.

TOO ROMANTIC

The relationship may be too romantic:

The Greeks regarded the state of 'being in love' as a form of madness and it is difficult to romanticise about being mad! In the West, however, we have valued a more exalted and romantic view of love. Emerson said, 'All mankind loves a lover', and history and literature are full of tales of passionate love affairs, unrequited love and lovers' suicide pacts. In recent years, the film *Love Story* dwelt intensively, and some feel nauseatingly, on the romanticism of young love.

We may feel better after a good tug on the heart-strings, but this sort of starry-eyed, head in the clouds state must come down to earth sooner or later. In the *Merchant of Venice* we read, 'But love is blind and lovers cannot see the pretty follies that themselves commit'. Love often is blind, but at some stage people who are striving for maturity and who are in love will need to put on glasses and focus on the loved one a little more sharply.

TOO PHYSICAL

Being in love can be clouded by a strong dose of romanticism; it can also be muddied by being too physical, by 'bedding before wedding':

For the last seventy years or so, Freudian attitudes about sex have held the stage. The argument goes like this: sex is an instinct, and instincts need satisfying. A girl student once said to me, "Surely, it's always right to give. If he wants it, I give it!" Here the view of sex is reduced to the simple instinctual level, equating "I want sex, I therefore have sexual intercourse" with "I want food, I therefore tuck into a steak".

It is interesting how ways of talking about these things reflect the shift in attitudes. Not so long ago, people talked of sexual intercourse with phrases like 'sleeping together' or 'making love'. Today, certainly among students, 'sleeping together' tends to mean simply sleeping together, perhaps naked, but at least without the intention of sexual intercourse. What was once described as 'making love' becomes 'having sex' and a girlfriend or boyfriend becomes a 'sexual partner'. This use of different words reflects the move from loving a person to loving *it*. Such contemporary attitudes are shown well in this peom by Steve Turner, *Tonight we will Fake Love:*

Tonight, we will
fake love together.
You my love, possess
all the essential qualities
as listed by Playboy.
You will last me for
as long as two weeks
or until such a time
as your face & figure
go out of fashion.
I will hold you close
to my Hollywood-standard body,
the smell of which
has been approved
by my ten best friends
and a representative
of Lifebuoy.
I will prop my paperback
Kama Sutra
on the dressing table
& like programmed seals
we will perform
& like human beings
we will grow tired
of our artificially sweetened
diluted & ready to drink
love affairs.

Tonight, we will fake love.
Tonight we will be both
quick & silent, our time limited,
measured out in distances
between fingers
        & pushbuttons.[2]

"So what?" many of the young people we are trying to help may say. "If you are in love then sexual intercourse is a natural development! What's the problem?" I remember one young woman in her mid-twenties, who had a series of what she described as stable relationships with A, B and then C, each involving sexual intercourse. D came along, proposed marriage and,

2. Turner, Steve. *Tonight We Will Fake Love* (Charisma Books, 1974) p. 15

although it seemed that he was ideal for her, she could not make a decision. She told me that the memories of A, B and C haunted their lovemaking.

Briefly, let us see what light is thrown on this issue by the Bible:

(a) As we saw in the last chapter, there were very few single girls at large in biblical days; and so the distinction drawn between adultery (a wrongful sexual union between a married person and someone else) and fornication (sexual intercourse between unmarried people) is not always clear in the Scriptures.

(b) Also we need to see that the Bible describes different degrees of sexual sin. In Deuteronomy we read of different punishments for a range of varied sexual sins. For example, under Old Testament law, adultery would lead to death for *both* parties; rape would be punished by death for the man; and fornication (in this instance where the man and woman were not pledged in marriage) would lead to the fine of 50 pieces of silver to the woman's father and then the dire punishment of marriage to the girl concerned!

(c) With these two points in mind, we must also see that the Bible condemns what today we call 'pre-marital intercourse'. In the Old Testament, this is alluded to in the assumption that a girl is a virgin at the start of marriage. In the New Testament, Paul argues powerfully in 1 Corinthians 6 on the same theme. He says that if we are Christians then our bodies are the Lord's, 'members of Christ', and 'temples of the Holy Spirit'. Further, sexual union, in this case with a prostitute (but more generally where God has not joined together) is sin. It is sin, says Paul, both against our own bodies and also against the God whose we are. 'The body is not for lust, but for the Lord,' he states in verse 13. Thirdly, the key is in our commitment to him. We are his. Paul says 'you do not belong to yourselves'. He has bought us with the price of his Son's death. 'Then, honour God in your body', he concludes. The logic is relentless!

Helen Lee underlined the continuing relevance of Paul's words when she said that there is a 'great tendency among young people to use their bodies not as a temple, but as an amusement arcade'.[3]

TO MARRY OR NOT?

And so we have our two single people very much in love and trying to steer a middle course between being too romantic and

3. Lee, Helen. *The Troubled Years* (Falcon, 1968) p. 84

being too physical in their friendship. If the relationship stands the test of time, sooner or later the question of marriage will arise.

Commitment for life is a daunting prospect. What guidelines could we offer when trying to help a single person with what can be an agonising decision? Before we consider these, let me emphasise the need for a sense of responsibility in this area. Many would-be advisors are shunned because they adopt a joking and insensitive manner towards the couple involved. On the other hand, we do our friends a great service when we help them sort out their feelings and thinking concerning their potential life-partners.

TOO IDEALISTIC?

A common mistake is to be too idealistic about the one you

love. People in love *do* believe that the other person is mind-shattering in every way and this marriage will be *the* marriage of the century.

Every day-dreaming man wants a woman who is attractive, has a beautiful figure, a quick mind, is a good conversationalist and an excellent cook. Every day-dreaming woman wants a man who is tall, handsome and muscular, who has a good sense of humour, is intelligent, is a do-it-yourself expert and earns lots of money. These thoughts are the stuff of day-dreams but they are not much help for day-to-day living:

BE REALISTIC

In helping single people with such a decision, we may need to seek lovingly to disillusion them and to encourage them towards realism. It probably will not make any difference, but we may need to try!

Way before the dizzy state of being in love, some Christian young men seem to find themselves in a special dilemma. Their reasoning seems to go something like this: "I want to marry the right one. I do not want to make a mistake. Therefore, I will keep well clear of girls until I know who the right one is!" Now imagine trying to buy a motor bike, a washing machine or a house in that sort of way! One may understand this circular thinking but it is far from realistic.

Further, in helping a young person who is in love and is trying to decide about this fantastic friend they have discovered, we need to urge him or her to think and pray and to ask down-to-earth questions, such as, "Would I like her to be the mother of my children?" "Do I find him interesting as a person?" "Will I still love her when she is vomiting into the loo early in pregnancy?" "Can I live with the noisy way he eats apples?"

Behind questions like these lie more fundamental considerations. These include: "What are our attitudes towards relatives, friends, potential neighbours, home-making, money, children, careers and ambitions?" "If we are at loggerheads in important areas like these, how will we handle our differences?" "What things do we enjoy doing together?" "Is there enough variety and depth of interest to give us sufficient common ground in our appreciation of life?" "What qualities attract me in the other person?" "Are they sufficient to give a firm basis to marriage?" "What features irritate me in the other person?" "Can I adjust to these irritations?"

Behind all such considerations, there are the fundamental issues for the Christian: "Are we one in the Lord?" "Do we both want God's ways?" "Do we both want him to be the centre of the marriage?" Here, as elsewhere, there is great need for caution. The point was well made in an anonymous article published by Scripture Union:

'The acceptance of Christ as Saviour by two people who subsequently get married is no guarantee that Christ is therefore Lord, either of themselves or their marriage. A soldier is a soldier from the day he enlists but it may take a long time before he learns discipline and is steady under fire. A Christian, that is, a Christ-centred, marriage is often a very different thing from a marriage of two Christian people.'[4]

It is esential that the engaged couple see their coming marriage as a *reasonable* risk! Their commitment must be realistic and their reasons for marrying be understood. Every marriage has an element of risk, of uncertainty as to exactly how it will work out. It is all the more important for the couple to be able to look back at their decision-making and their vows before God when the marriage is going through a sticky patch.

In the West, we put a very high premium on not only falling in love, but also on making the right choices for marriage. In the last chapter we will consider how these attitudes can create special problems which threaten the stability of certain marriages. I remember a converted Hindu from India saying something like this, "In the West, you start hot with your love-matches and then become cold; in the East, we start cold and then become hot, because we have to work at our arranged marriages."

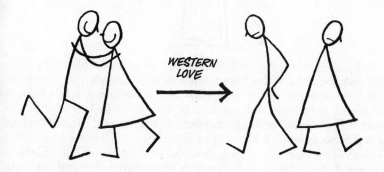

WESTERN
LOVE

4. Anon. *Outreach* (Scripture Union, April/June 1973) p. 5

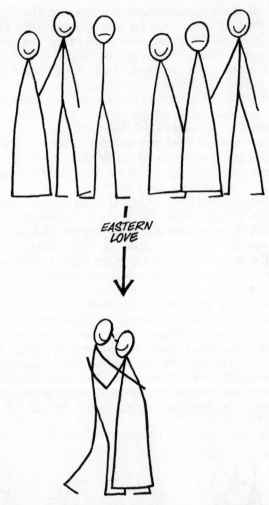

EASTERN
LOVE

Whatever our approach to the idea of wedded bliss, the bliss can only be achieved where a great deal is put into the marriage. It is interesting to reflect that Isaac had it both ways! His was an arranged marriage and yet it was also love at first sight. We read, "Then Isaac brought her into the tent, and took Rebekah and she became his wife; and he loved her." (Genesis 24:67 RSV) However, even with this double guarantee of an Eastern arranged marriage and a Western love-match, he and his wife were at loggerheads about their formidable sons not many years later!

Samuel Butler said this about Thomas Carlyle's marriage, "It was very good of God to let Mr. and Mrs. Carlyle marry each other. It meant only two people were made miserable instead of four."!

It is examples like these that should remind us to encourage people considering marriage to be realistic!

MARRIAGE

There are many contrary views about marriage and family life in our society. Someone has described marriage as 'a foretaste of heaven or an anticipation of hell'. Others regard the family as a thoroughly bad influence. Dr. Edmund Leach once said, in the Reith Lectures of 1967, "Far from being the basis of a good society, the Family, with its narrow privacy and tawdry secrets, is the source of all our discontents." More healthily (for it's always good to laugh at ourselves) marriage is often the butt of a humour about blown fuses, blocked drains and mothers-in-law. Sarah, when she was twelve, came home one day and said, "Here's a good one, Dad — 'Marriage starts when you sink in his arms; it ends with your arms in his sink!' "

Germaine Greer developed this line of thinking in her book *The Female Eunuch:* 'Every wife must live with the knowledge that she has nothing else but home and family, while her house is ideally a base which her tired warrior-hunter can withdraw to and express his worst manners, his least amusing conversation, while he licks his wounds and is prepared by laundry and toilet and lunch-box for another sortie.'[5]

These then are some of our modern views on 'wedded bliss' — some whimsically hopeful, others disillusioned and cynical. We need now to consider the Biblical foundation of marriage if we are going to help married people towards responsibility, fulfilment and Christian maturity. Throughout this handbook, we have found ourselves in Genesis 1 and 2 and this chapter is no exception, as it is here that we see that marriage was an essential part of God's master plan for men and women given before the Fall. In understanding this Order of Creation, we see three main aspects of what it means to be a man and a woman made by God.

EQUAL

First, men and women are equal. 'Then God said, "Let us make man in our image, after our likeness . . ." '; and it is

5. Greer, Germaine. *The Female Eunuch* (Paladin, 1970) p. 232

because man is made in God's image, that there is a deep desire for someone else. The nature of God is to love and to give; we are made in His image and we therefore desire to love and to give. Loving and giving require others to love and give to, and so we read in Genesis 1:27: 'Male and female he created them'.

We could simplify this point by saying that God is Three in One and is a trinity. Man is two in one: a bi-unity. And, as the three persons are equal within the Trinity, so man and woman are equal within their bi-unity. Male and female together, constitute 'man'. Someone has commented on this; 'Male and female created he them and called their name (*not* names) Adam (and *not* the Adamses)'.

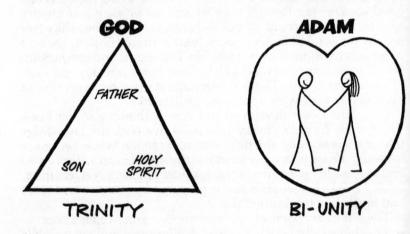

From this we see that the Bible does not regard woman as a second class citizen. The Ancient Greeeks did (see the next diagram).

Augustine was being more Greek than Christian when he said, "We must look upon the female character as being a sort of natural deficiency." Many other Christians before and since have made the same mistake. Una Kroll, in her book *Flesh of my Flesh*, tells how, while she was carrying her fourth child and wandering in a church, she overheard a priest say, "The sight of a pregnant woman in the sanctuary of the church is a blasphemy, an insult to God". And as a result of this, she says, she wrote her book. In *Flesh of my Flesh* she mentions a line of her favourite prayer: "I will call you brother, even though you will not call me sister".

Colin Morris was well aware of Genesis 1 and 2 when, at a rally of 5,000 women at the Albert Hall in 1975 (Women's International Year), he said, "We don't have to make women equal to men; God has already done so". This equality is beautifully shown in Genesis 2:21 and 22 where we read that 'woman came from a rib taken from man's side'. Matthew Henry's commentary on this is well known but is worth repeating:

'The woman was made out of a rib out of the side of Adam;
not made out of his head to rule over him
nor out of his feet to be trampled on by him,
but out of his side to be equal with him,
under his arm to be protected, and near his heart to be loved.'

Although the Women's Lib Movement has done a tremendous amount of good in waking us up to unjust attitudes and structures as far as women are concerned, some of its advocates have seemed to want a reversal of roles. We can caricature these three views about men and women as follows:

GREEK

WOMEN'S LIB

We have already seen that the Lord Jesus went against the attitudes of the time with regard to women. We see him courteous, caring and loving towards the Samaritan woman at the well, in the healing of the daughter of the Canaanite woman, in relation to Mary Magdalene, and so on. These interactions were a complete flouting of the laws of the community in which he lived.

Paul, much misunderstood on the subject of women, said at the opening of the section on husbands and wives in Ephesians 5: 'Be subject to one another, out of reverence for Christ'. And in 1 Corinthians 11:11 and 12, he wrote, 'Nevertheless in the Lord woman is not independent of man nor man of woman; for as woman was made from man, so man is now born of woman. And all things are from God'. Both Our Lord and Paul, then, in their attitudes and words, seem to agree with the essential equality between men and women that we have seen in the first two chapters of Genesis.

With some trepidation, I would like to write something about the controversial subject of what it means for the man to be the *head* of the marriage in relation to man and woman being equal. There are still many marriages, particularly amongst Christians, where a mistaken view of headship has lead to a crushing domination in the husband's attitudes and behaviour, mirrored by a pitiful servility on the part of his wife. We will come across situations like this in our counselling and it is therefore worthwhile spending a little time considering this question.

There is not the space to look in detail at what Paul said about women, but there is no doubt that he and other church leaders had their problems with certain Christian women who were experiencing a new freedom in Christ. It seems that they were dominating discussions, took pride in disagreeing with their husbands in public gatherings, and were even leaving their husbands. There was an excessive bid for freedom from these liberated first century women, liberated in Christ. Some, apparently, were bent on usurping the men and seizing authority.

Basically, Paul was trying to remind such Christian women that God is a God of order. 1 Corinthians 11 exemplifies this reasoning. In 1 Corinthians 11:3 we read these difficult words. 'But I (Paul) want you to understand that the head of every man is Christ, the head of a woman is her husband, and the head of Christ is God.' At a quick reading, this seems to suggest that men are by nature superior to women. But if we say that, we must also conclude from the passage that God is *by nature superior to Christ*, and this is clearly nonsense. Paul's meaning clearly rests on the sense in which the word 'head' was used. In the Greek it has here the sense of 'beginning' or 'origin' rather than 'lord' or 'master' and therefore we could rephrase this passage as Olthuis does, 'Without Christ from out of whom and in relation to whom man exists, there is no man. Without man out of whom and in relation to whom woman exists, there is no woman. Without God from whom and in relation to whom Christ exists, there is no Christ'.[6] This, we see, fits in with the account in Genesis. Headship in marriage, then, is not as in Robert Burns' words:

'Husband, husband, cease your strife,
No longer idly rave, sir.
Though I am your wedded wife,
Yet I am not your slave, sir.'

The husband is *not* the boss; he is the head simply in the sense of having the prime responsibility and authority to call both himself and his wife to obey God's will for marriage.

In Genesis 2 the equality of man and woman is described more poetically. We see Adam the gardener, enjoying the perfect surroundings and the good produce of the garden, relaxed and open before the Lord God, his Creator. And yet we read, 'The Lord God said, "It is not good".' What is this? "*Not* good"? We have read in Genesis 1 that God says of all that he made, "It is good" or "It is very good". Let us read on in verse 18 of chapter 2: "It is not good *that the man should be alone*; I will make him a helper fit for him". And so, out of the ground, the Lord God made every beast of the field and bird of the air. We

6. Olthuis, James H. *I Pledge You My Troth* (Harper & Row, 1975) p. 137

can imagine all the beautiful, strange and powerful creatures of the Animal Kingdom there before him, *but* 'there was not found a helper fit for him'.

Then, we read, a deep sleep came upon Adam, a rib was taken and so woman was made and brought to him. As someone has said, "They came to each other from each other". If the man did not leap in the air at this stage, there was certainly a leap in his voice: "This *at last* is bone of my bones and flesh of my flesh; she shall be called Woman because she was taken out of Man".

FOR EACH OTHER

First, we have seen that men and women are equal and now we think about woman as a 'help-meet' or 'help-mate'. This can be variously restated as : 'a helper meet', 'one adapted to', 'one who perfectly complements' and 'a helper as opposite to'. In the 1662 Prayer Book, the Marriage Service gives three reasons for marriage. One of them is: 'For the mutual society, help and comfort one of the other'. Also the Old English word 'troth' is used in the commitment of the husband to the wife and vice versa, using the quaint phrase, 'And thereto I plight thee my troth'. The word 'troth' includes the ideas of truth, faithfulness, loyalty and honesty, and these are central to the very idea of marriage.[7]

So many relationships between men and women today are like the one in this poem by Steve Turner where there is no understanding of troth, *Declaration of Intent:*

> She said she'd
> love me for eternity
> but managed to reduce
> it to eight months
> for good behaviour.
> She said we fitted
> like a hand in a glove
> but then the hot
> weather came and such
> accessories weren't needed.
> She said the future
> was ours but the deeds
> were made out in
> her name.
> She said I was
> the only one who
> understood completely
>
> and then she left me
> and said she knew
> that I'd understand completely.[8]

In contrast, the biblical pattern for marriage is about mutual helping, caring, sharing and self-giving love for a life time, as in 1 Peter 3: 'Wives be submissive to your husbands, . . . have the hidden person of the heart with the imperishable jewel of a gentle and quiet spirit, which in God's sight is very precious'. We can imagine the husbands sitting back a little smugly at this stage as they read Peter's letter. However, he goes on, 'Husbands, live considerately with your wives'. Here is a challenge for the men, because 'considerately' involves thought, anticipation and understanding. Is the sort of considerate, self-giving love that the Bible talks about, easy? Many of us know the sort of situations where such fine talk and fine feelings seem to fly out through the window:

Wife (in kitchen, looking at clock)	He's late again! The meal is spoilt. I bet it's that secretary . . . !

7. Olthuis, James H. op. cit. p. 21, etc.
8. Turner, Steve. op. cit. p. 28

| *Husband* (at wheel of car in traffic jam) | I feel really tired with all this extra work. Dash, it's getting really late! Never mind, there'll be a good meal when I get back . . . then there's the telly. Yes, it'll be after eight by the time I get in and she'll have put the kids to bed! |

Husband arrives home, puts the car in the garage, walks up the drive, turns the key in the door and enters.

| *Wife* | Where have YOU been? |
| *Husband* (with wide-eyed innocence) | To work, darling! |

Wife is speechless while husband enters the lounge, switches on the box, yawns and settles in the most comfortable armchair. Husband is vaguely conscious of oven-door slamming in the background; seconds later he hears another noise . . .

| *Husband* | Could it be a broken plate? Funny! The programme's finished and still no food. I'm hungry. |

Husband wanders into the kitchen, still clutching the TV Times. His wife is sobbing uncontrollably.

| *Husband* (can think of nothing but . . .) | How silly she looks, all pink and blotchy! |

How difficult it can be living together, 'for each other', in love and consideration. What might be the outcome of this sort of kitchen sink drama? Three days' silence? Angry outbursts in which they throw every resentment and unhappy memory at each other? A fumbling attempt to understand each other and apologise?

DIFFERENT

We considered the glorious fact that men and women are different in the last chapter and echoed the Frenchman's, "Vive la différence".

So from Genesis we see that men and women are equal, made for each other and are essentially different. More briefly, we must now consider the themes of Leaving, Cleaving and One Flesh, all integral to a maturing marriage. To do this, let us look at three statements made in Genesis 2:24 and 25.

Leaving — 'A man leaves his father and his mother'

In trying to help others who have problems in their marriages, we may find that the root of the difficulty is the failure of one or both partners truly to 'leave' their parents.

Nowadays, with the great mobility of our society, it is common for married couples to be at least one or two hundred miles from their respective parents. At times they are frankly grateful, recalling the lines of the hymn, 'Peace, perfect peace, with loved ones far away'! Even so, there are many new marriages where the pull back to Mum and Dad is very strong. I remember a Christian engaged couple I knew some time ago where trouble seemed to loom ahead. He was attached to Mum in a deeply emotional way, and although a grown man, he described himself as 'Mum's little boy', his eyes softening at the thought. There were rows already and in these Mum always came off best and never his fiancée. I felt that he would have great difficulty in 'leaving'.

Less often these days, the married couple's parents live nearby and this can be a source of strife. Jenny has never had a baby of her own and Mrs. Brown, her mother, had 'such a dreadful time' with hers, that she is determined to hold Jenny's hand throughout. Little Amanda is perfect, just like Jenny was, and not a bit like her husband, David. As time slips by, David wonders whether he married Jenny, her mother, Mrs. Brown, or neither!

As always, there is a great need for balance, which may take time to establish. The mature marriage is able to relate to the parents on both sides in a new adult way. This means that the parents will be happy for the new unit to find its own level, and yet, will be happy to advise and help where appropriate. The newly-weds will enjoy learning by trial and error but will be glad of help on occasions. This mutual caring and respect for each family unit can lead to an enriched form of extended family.

Cleaving — 'And cleaves to his wife'

To cleave is to weld, to adhere tightly, to grip, to be separation-proof. Some years ago there was a tragedy in our family. I rarely break things but when I do, I do it properly. We had been given a large Victorian Wedgwood cheese-dish by a fond aunt, and I dropped it! The various classical figures were painstakingly joined together again with Araldite; now nothing can separate them. And the Bible says that in one sense marriage should be like that. Like the restored cheese-dish, it should be separation-proof, distinguished by 'to love and to cherish till one of us perish'.

This should not be, on the one hand, the sort of exclusivist marriage mentioned in Chapter Three, where the couples are 'in each other's pockets', always hand in hand, and endlessly looking into each other's eyes. Married couples need other friends and others need them.

On the other hand, there is one area where the marriage must be exclusivist and that is at the most intimate sexual level. Hebrews 13:4 makes the point clearly: 'Let the marriage bed be undefiled; for God will judge the immoral and adulterous'.

In the last chapter we will look at this matter of cleaving, and not cleaving, more thoroughly as we look at 'Lean-to' marriages, 'I've made a Mistake' marriages, the Seven Year Itch, and the Eternal Triangle.

Becoming One Flesh — 'Therefore a man leaves his father and his mother and cleaves to his wife, and they become one flesh.'

The 'one flesh' relationship between a man and a woman is mentioned many times in the Bible and is regarded as the very essence of marriage, in which there is marrying together of two to become one. We read that Adam and Eve were 'both naked and not ashamed' and this brings us to the third main theme of marriage, sexual intercourse. It is interesting that no children are mentioned in Genesis 2, and to see sex only in terms of having children is an injustice towards God's good gift. In the next chapter we will allow our married couple to have or to adopt lots of children, but not yet!

We see something of the joy of sexual union in this song by Tom Paxton:

'When we were good she had her way with me
She'd simply stay with me,
And make my whole day ring.
When we were good she'd make the nights go fast;
She'd put out the lights so fast,
She made my body sing.
Oh! She knew me inside out.
Oh! She made my senses shout . . .'

The Bible is also unashamedly positive about God's good gift of sex. We see the man's view in Proverbs 5:

'Find joy with the wife you married in your youth,
Fair as a hind, graceful as a fawn.
Let hers be the company you keep,
Hers the breasts that ever fill you with delight,
Hers the love that ever holds you captive.'

We see the woman's view in the Song of Songs 2:1-6:

'He took me into the wine-garden and gave me loving glances,
He refreshed me with raisins,
He revived me with apricots,
For I was faint with love;
His left arm was under my head, his right arm was round me.'

Sex is not the be-all and end-all of marriage, but physical love is essential and needs care, understanding and a sense of humour. On this last point, C. S. Lewis wrote that with regard to sex, 'Nothing is more needed than a roar of old-fashioned laughter'.[9] Some years ago there was a letter published in the Church of England Newspaper from a curate who was expressing his view on what he would most look for in a wife-to-be. He was being scriptural, as well as honest, when he wrote that she should be 'eminently bedworthy'!

Like all good things, sex can be misused in marriage. John enjoyed sex early in their married life, reaching his climax quickly. Meg never seemed quite to get there. She said that she did not mind and so John gave up trying to arouse her. He became lazy and selfish and never cared enough to learn the art of making love.

Maria had the upper hand. She knew that Bruce was crazy about her. Well, he had not put those shelves up yet so he would not 'get any' tonight!

9. Lewis, C. S. op. cit.p. 91

Paul shows that self-giving not self-witholding is the hall-mark of erotic love, as in all other aspects of trothful marriage. We see this in 1 Corinthians 7:3-5, 'The husband should give to his wife her conjugal rights and likewise the wife to her husband. For the wife does not rule over her own body, but the husband does; likewise the husband does not rule over his own body, but the wife does. Do not refuse one another . . .' Paul reluctantly allows one temporary exception here, 'Do not refuse one another except perhaps by agreement for a season, that you may devote yourselves to prayer. But then', he adds, '*come together again*'.

There is little space here to follow Adam and Eve closely. They did not walk away into the setting sun holding hands, with the strings of Mantovani in the background. Their dis-obedience and rebellion spoilt the story; their troth was pro-foundly shaken. Adam blamed his wife and she blamed the serpent. Guilty and embarrassed by their nakedness, they hid themselves from the Lord God. The disorder of the Fall followed the order of Creation.

The Lord God talked to them of the coming pain of child-birth; of the twist in the husband/wife relationship towards him becoming a bully and the woman becoming a cringing slave; of the back-breaking work of the hard years ahead. This looked ominously like a shift from marriage being a partnership to being a prison (see Genesis 3:16-19)!

And yet, Adam and Eve did not split up although the contrast between Eden and the harsh, fallen world must have been appalling. They had problems! They had children! One of their sons even murdered his brother!

And so it is for us and those we try to help. We cannot side-step the demands of life. We cannot avoid the hard work and the difficult situations. Someone has said, "It takes three to make a marriage"; here we are not thinking of the notorious third party who comes in and upsets the marriage, but of the Lord God himself, working in marriages by his spirit, making both individuals and couples more mature and Christ-like. There can be a glorious restoration of marriage according to principles laid down before the Fall.

We have considered the biblical foundation for marriage. Let us now turn our attention to marital counselling.

MARITAL COUNSELLING

Much of what I have written will I hope be useful to us as we face up to our own marriages and as we try to help our friends with marital difficulties. As before, we need to keep in mind the principles of Involvement, Responsibility, and Right and Wrong, in our caring. Again, there is discussion material at the end of the chapter which could be worked through profitably either individually or in groups.

Let us now consider briefly three main patterns of helping marriages in difficulty.

ONE TO ONE

Although Jesus had the discernment to challenge the woman at the well concerning the fact that she had many husbands, it is not ideal for us to try to help a married friend with his or her marital difficulties when only half of the 'one-flesh unit' is present.

However, it is not unusual to find a situation where one will come for help but the other will not. Quite often, it is the woman who comes; she may be desperately unhappy, she may spend long, long hours with bickering small children as her only company and she may then pass wretched evenings and nights with a man with whom she has fallen out of love, or at least out of communication. He too may be at his wit's end, but the busy structuring of his day working with others and his intense weariness at facing his family of sorry reminders in the evening may deter him from talking about the marriage with anyone.

One of the biggest pitfalls in counselling just half of the marriage is the temptation to take sides. It is so easy to find oneself thinking, "What a blackguard he must be to treat her like that!" or "What a woman to go on and on so!" In the second situation one may be reminded of the line in Proverbs, 'A continual dripping on a rainy day and a contentious woman are alike'. "No wonder he's a nervous wreck," we may quickly reflect. (See diagram on page 94). It is much wiser to reserve judgement and keep an open mind towards the absent partner.

Sometimes one spouse will talk well and find your caring helpful. He or she might then in turn be encouraged to persuade the other partner to come too. If this does not happen, then the man or woman who has been to see you will need to try responsibly on the domestic front in the spirit of the wife described in 1 Peter 3 mentioned in page 87.

ONE TO TWO

Although it is probably best to see each partner of a marriage individually at first, there will come a time quite quickly when it will be more helpful to see them together.

When we first came to Bristol in 1969 I worked as a part-time assistant in the Department of Mental Health and found sessions trying to help married couples together both hair-raising and worthwhile. The consulting rooms in the old Out Patients were tiny and the walls fairly reverberated with emotions generated and released as the three of us sat almost knee to knee! As Christians who care we may find this form of counselling specially demanding. However, where there is a loving involvement and a good sprinkling of the qualities we mentioned in our first chapter, we may well find that the sweat and tears are worthwhile for the couple involved. Some will ask, "What is the point of allowing two people in difficulty to repeat their battles in the presence of a third person?" What is the place of a scene like this (see below) as part of our Christian caring?

I suggest that the aims of this *One to Two* counselling are:

(a) If the couple can react with each other in your presence, you may be able to help them understand *why* they bridle so readily and then *how* they might begin to overcome their difficulties. So often, a couple fights tooth and nail because the levels of communication are blocked, something like this:

I UNDERSTAND ME
HE DOESN'T UNDERSTAND ME
I DON'T UNDERSTAND HIM

I UNDERSTAND ME
SHE DOESN'T UNDERSTAND ME
I DON'T UNDERSTAND HER

Perhaps, in our imaginary couple, she feels that he always ignores her in company; perhaps he feels that he is the life and soul of the party and that the guests need his brilliant conversation. It will help her to see that he is not being intentionally rude towards her. It will help him to understand that she feels hurt because he is being a bit of a bore. If you like, the aim of all this is to move in the direction where she can say, "I understand me, and he understands me, and I understand him", and he can make the same observations from his point of view:

I UNDERSTAND ME
HE UNDERSTANDS ME
I UNDERSTAND HIM

I UNDERSTAND ME
SHE UNDERSTANDS ME
I UNDERSTAND HER

(b) Having achieved a new measure of understanding as to why and how they hurt each other, the themes of Responsibility and Right and Wrong will come up. This will often mean mutual apologies and forgiveness as the injunction 'Do not let the sun go down on your wrath' has probably been forgotten long ago by the married couple, indeed if it was ever learnt by them. Pride can be very deeply rooted and this may well be a difficult step.

(c) Mutual understanding may be beginning, forgiveness may have been offered and accepted and now there is the need to _show_ their love for each other on a day to day basis. There is real progress when he stops lovingly to include her in the conversation. There is real progress when she finds that her resentment has gone.

We have thought about small everyday issues but it is amazing how many declining relationships begin their difficulties with quite modest misunderstandings, leading to a cycle of resentment, unforgiveness and non-communication.

GROUPS

Sometimes it will be helpful for two married couples to share their difficulties. Very often it is _one_ of the two groups who is in the greater need at the time, but this situation could easily be reversed six months later! This probably works best where the four people involved are good friends and find that they can share readily when appropriate.

If the two couples are comparative strangers, then it can be difficult to keep the main line of enquiry and the challenge of responsibility at the right pitch. The two counselling may find themselves pulling the other two in opposite directions! However, this sort of misunderstanding can be turned to give helpful insight for all four people involved.

Today, group experience is something that many of us are being urged to take part in. Tupperware parties have given way to T-groups, encounter groups and creativity workshops. Gestalt therapy and Transactional Analysis are household words to some, while amongst Christians Clinical Theology is the subject of a great deal of discussion.

There is no doubt that we are made for one another and many have been helped to a greater understanding of themselves in groups like these. If these insights are harnessed in a positive way, then marriages and other relationships can move into greater maturity.

Perhaps the burgeoning of group involvements and group therapies highlights the poor quality of much Christian fellowship, which should after all be the richest form of group experience! How often do we go back to our homes or out into our jobs from meeting with other Christians feeling enriched, strengthened and ready for the realities of our relationships, work and leisure?

Nevertheless, house groups and other forms of meeting together can be very helpful especially as people get to know one another and can begin to share. The inter-change during an evening may lead later to such comments between a couple as, "Do you think Miss Bloggs was right when she said that married people are too preoccupied with their children to really care about the elderly?" or "Why do you always sit next to Maximillian at the house group?" Interactions like these may lead to fresh understanding (or fresh misunderstanding) between them.

Joy and I are involved in a group of five Christian couples from four or five different fellowships who have been meeting periodically for a number of years. The original intention was one of outreach to business and professional people mainly, and this would involve a talk and a discussion on a topical subject following a good meal. We saw all this as part of our continuing friendship and caring for others. Out of this we have also seen the need to share between the ten of us, so that all of us would agree that we have learnt a great deal as a group, as married partners and as individuals as we look back over a number of years. There has been no deliberate attempt to sort ourselves out, but this type of thing will happen in small groups which meet regularly, especially if Christian maturity is a high priority.

CONCLUSION

Marriage is difficult, like all worthwhile things. It is an ordinance of God and can be a deeply enriching relationship for the couple involved. Where any two people try to live together for a lifetime, problems as well as pleasures will arise, and you and I may well be called on to listen and to try to help. We need to remember the stamp that Our Lord put upon the Creation order of marriage when he was asked a question about divorce (Matthew 19:3-6): "Have you not read that He who made them from the beginning made them male and female, and said, 'For this reason a man shall leave his father and mother and be joined to his wife, and the two shall become one'? So they are no longer two but one. What therefore God has joined together, let no man put asunder."

FOR DISCUSSION

Wilberforce and Wilhelmina have been married for five years, have a daughter, Wendy (two-and-a-half) and are expecting a second child in four months' time. They are Christians and both come from committed Christian backgrounds.

Wilberforce, an only son, works for an insurance company and this involves him in a fair amount of travelling; occasionally he has to be away, but rarely for more than two consecutive nights. He is heavily involved at the local church, is on many committees there and is also the leader of a boys' Bible Class. He is also quite a gifted speaker and is in much demand. Wilhelmina comes from a large family; she is a trained teacher but she has not taught since her first pregnancy.

You have always regarded them as a 'model couple'. You met Wilhelmina in the street the other day struggling along with a tearful Wendy. In conversation, she asked whether she might have a chat with you about something on her mind. You were able to have coffee together later and learned the following.

Wilhelmina is very unhappy and seems to doubt whether Wilberforce really loves her. She feels that he is staying out more and more. He comes home later from the office, explaining that the workload is increasing. He is also out most evenings and much of Sunday with church commitments, although she appears not to resent this. On a regular basis she only makes a Family Service with or without Wilberforce. She is full of self-recrimination, feels that she is going to seed intellectually and says that she is no longer attractive. She says that she doesn't enjoy their sex life and quickly adds that 'there are more important things in life'. She doesn't think that Wilberforce will admit to there being any problems in the marriage.

(1) Do you feel angry with Wilberforce or Wilhelmina?

  If so, what do you feel angry about?
  What would you like to say to one or other?
  What does this teach you about your own feelings?

(2) What are the possible reasons for Wilhelmina's unhappiness?

  A frustrated teacher?
  A worn-out mother?
  A love-starved wife?
  Any others?

(3) If you cannot see Wilberforce, how would you advise Wilhelmina?

> To support his Christian work?
> Tell him about her fears?
> Battle on doggedly?
> How else?

(4) If you could see Wilberforce, how would you advise him?

> That his wife is going through a phase?
> To give up some Christian work?
> That he is an irresponsible husband?
> That you would like to see them together?
> How else?

(As with the two earlier discussions, you may like to handle this material in other ways. If you are in a group, then you have a good opportunity to act in a kitchen-sink drama! Wilberforce has come home late from the office, his dinner has been spoiled and he is about to rush out to yet another church meeting. Wilhelmina has forgotten about this meeting and has set her heart on talking things over with Wilberforce on this particular evening. In this scene you can really let the sparks fly and a lively and useful discussion should follow.

Again, it could be very instructive for different members of the group to attempt interviews with Wilhelmina, Wilberforce, and then the couple together.)

FOR FURTHER READING

Dobson, J. *Man to Man About Women* (Coverdale House) 1976

Lewis, C. S. *The Four Loves* (London, Collins/Fontana) 1960

Miles, H. J. *Sexual Happiness in Marriage* (Grand Rapids, Zondervan) 1967

Miles, H. J. *Sexual Understanding Before Marriage* (Grand Rapids, Zondervan) 1971

Olthuis, J. *I Pledge You My Troth* (San Francisco, Harper and Row) 1975

Townsend, A. *Marriage without Pretending* (London, The Scripture Union) 1975

Trobisch, W. *I Married You* (Leicester, IVP) 1971

CHAPTER FIVE

Marital Counselling — Middle Years and beyond

In preparing this handbook, I have been aware that each chapter could be developed into a further small book and this final chapter is no exception. In thinking beyond the early years of marriage, we shall inevitably need to consider something of the wide spectrum of human experience. In *As You Like It*, Shakespeare writes, 'One man in his time plays many parts, His acts being seven ages'. In this chapter we shall need to include the first stage of 'the infant mewling and puking in the nurse's arms', and the seventh age of 'second childishness and mere oblivion', as well as a great deal between.[1] As a result, what I write will often be the merest outline of matters that are worthy of more thorough treatment.

FAMILY

In the last chapter we allowed our two single friends to fall in love and then take the 'reasonable risk' of marriage. We stressed that they were seeking to live together on the biblical principles of leaving, cleaving and 'one flesh'. We have given them very little time to learn to adjust to each other, and to allow their married relationship to begin to mature. In this chapter we will allow them to have children, and thus they are now a family!

FAMILY IN THE BIBLE

The concept of family has had many variations since the days of Adam, Eve, Cain and Abel, and it is instructive to consider briefly the idea of family in the Bible.

In chapter four we saw that the husband/wife relationship must come first in the biblical view, and that children are not mentioned in Genesis 2. However, in Genesis 1:28, we read what seems to me to be the most daunting command in the whole Bible: 'God said, "Be fruitful and multiply, and fill the earth and subdue it . . ."' We can imagine Adam and Eve quaking at the prospect of filling the earth with offspring!

1. Shakespeare, William. *As You Like It.* Act II, Scene vii

The Fall spoilt the beautiful, one to one, trothful relationship of Adam and Eve, and so we find many patterns of family in the rest of the Old Testament which reflect the twist in man's nature. For example, in the Patriarchal period polygamy was widely practised. The sort of heartbreak which developed is well known in the story of Elkanah and his two wives, Hannah and Peninnah. We read in 1 Samuel 1:6 that "Hannah's rival used to torment her and humiliate her because she had no children".

Such a childless wife as Hannah was regarded as a particular tragedy in the Old Testament era. One aspect of this was the giving of the wife's maidservant to her husband to produce the deeply desired children. Sarah's gift of Hagar, her Egyptian slave girl, to Abram is a familiar example of this arrangement (Genesis 16:1-4).

In these ways and others, we see that the woman had an inferior status in the lives of the ancient Jews. She was often chosen for marriage by the man's parents and her family was compensated by the bride-price. Basically a chattel, she could be divorced by her husband, but the reverse does not seem to have been possible (Deuteronomy 22:13; 24:1-4).

Another aspect of this polygamous society was the concubines who were second-rate wives obtained by purchase or by capture in times of war. Solomon took this to an extreme!

It is like a breath of clean, wholesome air when we turn to the New Testament and see the restoration of the Creation Order for marriage and family. The importance of family to God is shown in Paul's description of him as 'the Father, from whom every family in heaven and on earth is named' (Ephesians 3:14, 15).

The Greek word for family most frequently used in the New Testament is sometimes translated 'household'. This comprised not only the lord of the household, the master, his wife, children and slaves, but also other dependents, servants and employees. It is a picture reflected in the more affluent Victorian households that we may read about today. These 'extended families' were very important in the growth and stability of the church as centres of teaching, prayer, fellowship and worship. The Church itself is described as 'the household of God' in

Ephesians 2:19 RSV and the fact that the early Christians called themselves brothers and sisters emphasizes the closeness of relationships within God's family.

Within these crowded households were the 'nuclear families' made up of husband, wife and children, and, as we know, there is a great deal of wonderfully balanced instruction for these units in the New Testament especially in the writings of Paul and Peter (Ephesians 5:21-6:4; Colossians 3:18-21; 1 Peter 3:1-7).

FAMILY TODAY

First of all we have to see that family life today is threatened. In our western society, many of us have lost the sense of security and belonging that the extended family of the Bible, of history and of other cultures gives. It may be this sense of loss that has encouraged many, myself included, to take up an interest in family history. In so doing, one quickly sees that all was not sweetness and light! Hurdings, for example, were struggling to win a living off the land at the end of the eighteenth century and one whole family unit was moved by the authorities from one parish to another. A generation later, the sister-in-law of an ancestor had three base-born sons in a few years, all called George!

Today's nuclear family of husband, wife and 'two and a bit' children, has on the whole different influences moulding it than our ancestors had in their more extended families. These include great pressures towards isolation, towards being cut off from others. Sociologists have had a field day describing these factors and they are all real enough. Industrialisation and urbanisation have led to a greater mobility for contemporary families with all the uprooting that means. It would be quite interesting to know how many of the readers of this handbook are living within ten miles of where they were born. So much is provided for us in today's world in the way of education, health care, financial benefits and other facets of the welfare state, that we do not need the nurturing of family in these respects, unlike our ancestors. These and other factors have served to whittle down our extended families into small isolated units which are often self-contained, inward looking and often 'boxward looking'.

Along with these isolating factors are the many disruptive pressures of today's attitudes and today's morals. We saw in the last chapter how romanticism can be a shaky foundation for marriage. Family life is further threatened by the attitude of self-fulfilment, in which the individual *must* be fulfilled at all costs, even at the expense of others; and also by materialism, where things are more important than people.

In the face of these powerful influences, let us now consider today's family more positively. If we are going to help families in trouble, we need to see what ingredients can make family life a great recipe for joyful and realistic living.

In the autumn of 1976, while I was preparing a talk entitled 'What is a Family?' my wife Joy posed this question to Rachel who was then aged eight, and we also raised the same query with Simon (eleven), and Sarah (thirteen). Their replies reflect the differences in their personalities. Sarah in her matter of fact way said, "What is a family? Oh, that's the name of a book by Edith Schaeffer!" Simon, in poetic mood, thought for a while, and said, "A family is like a tree, because it's always growing", and Rachel, warm and outgoing, replied, "What is a family? Well, it's a group of people who love one another, of course!"

They were *all* right, but Rachel gave the main ingredient in the recipe of family life: love. This love has many qualities including affection, friendship and, supremely between husband and wife, erotic love. Over all this and enriching each quality is *agape*, the self-giving love, the caring, the love that God has for us, and that we can learn to have for one another.

Not all families, of course, have children. For some it is because the couple are still adjusting to each other and need more time for this. Some choose not to have children, giving preference to careers, to financial considerations, to decisions about an over-populated world, or simply for 'the quiet life'. Others find that they cannot have children of their own and these may consider adoption.

Those who do have children sometimes wonder where they went wrong, to have filled the house with sticky finger-marks, broken crockery, that special smell of unchanged nappies, the heart-rending cries of 'three month colic' and those early morning screams of a toddler with earache. Yet the Bible cheerfully says, "Happy is the man who has his quiver full of them!" What about these quiverfuls?

First, let us consider a few pitfalls common in the shaky ground of certain families.

(i) The husband/wife relationship must come *first*. It is no answer to try to solve the difficulties of a marriage by having children. It is not fair on the husband, wife, or children! In fact, the problems only increase. The husband becomes more and more ousted by the world of clucking mums, changing nappies and the preparation of feeds. His wife is now contented as her maternal instinct is being noisily fulfilled. The nights are disrupted and so she is too tired and preoccupied to make love. He becomes increasingly resentful and jealous of the intruder.

(ii) The dangers of favouritism were considered in chapter two in the story of Isaac and Rebekah. It is so easy to take sides, e.g. son says to father, "Dad, Mum says I can't go fishing." Father to son, "Does she? Just you wait here. I'll see to your Mum!" Dad wants to go fishing too.

(iii) Also in chapter two we saw the need for a truly Christian approach to discipline, avoiding the authoritarian, 'father is always right', parent-centred approach on the one hand, and avoiding the permissive, 'fun for all the family', child-centred approach on the other. (See pages 43 and 44.)

Olthuis in *I Pledge You My Troth* gives three very helpful pictures of what family life, or home, should be like.

Home is Rest.   The Shorter Oxford English Dictionary gives one definition of a *happy family* as 'a collection of birds and animals of different natures living together peaceably in one cage'. I do not think that this is quite the picture that Olthuis has in mind when he says that home is rest. He has rather the idea of *restfulness*, that home is where a child can relax and simply learn to be himself or herself. One of the most difficult things for parents is to accept their son or daughter as they are. This is not to deny the need to correct and train towards unselfishness and responsibility, but the issue is that of allowing children to be themselves. In my work as a doctor to students, I have seen many who at the age of eighteen or nineteen are still struggling to be, not themselves, but the brilliant sportsman or accomplished intellect that their parents have set their sights on.

The sad thing here and in many other instances is that parents have made their love conditional. The message to the child is something like this, although the words may not be spoken: "If you don't do this, then Mum won't love you", or "If you don't behave like that, then Dad won't love you". The child wants his or her parents' love but not with strings attached. This path can lead to uncertainty, to a fear of not being loved and even to misery.

An important part of encouraging children is to allow them

'emotional space', in which they can experience and express feelings without undue pressure or interference from outside. In this sense, home should be an undemanding place within which a child or adolescent can discover and be himself or herself.

The Bible gives the framework for home being a place where you can be yourself and where trust and security can be established. We see this in Ephesians 6 where the injunctions, 'Children, obey your parents in the Lord' and 'Honour your father and mother' signify the need for obedience and respect; and 'Fathers, do not provoke your children to anger but bring them up in the discipline and instruction of the Lord' points to the need for love, consideration and fairness, avoiding sarcasm, browbeating, nagging and emotional blackmail.

Home is Adventure.   Olthuis writes, 'The first priceless gift parents can give their children is roots. The second is wings'.[2] The nuclear family does not have to be isolated. There is the big wide world out there and it is God's world!

Parents do well when they can encourage their children to be neighbourly and have a social concern, as well as develop appetites for discovery and creativity. As parents, we have seen with new eyes the shape of a tree or a snail shell, or the colour of the sea or the sky, caught up by our children's enthusiasm. Edith Schaeffer in her book 'What is a Family?' rightly spends a great deal of space on 'Home as Adventure'.

Home is Guidance.   The scriptures are emphatic on the need to guide and discipline children. We read in Proverbs 13:24, 'He who spares the rod hates his son but he who loves him is diligent to discipline him' and in Proverbs 19:18, 'Discipline your son while there is hope; do not set your heart on his destruction'.

If we love our children, then we are to instruct them. Why? This is the way to life says the writer of Proverbs: 'Keep hold of instruction, do not let go; guard her, for she is your life' (Proverbs 4:13).

In all this, parents need to listen to their children too! It is so easy to make a judgement while ignoring all messages that we may be mistaken. For example, a child's obstinacy may be a cry for help rather than a challenge to parental authority.

We have seen throughout this book that the Fall affects every aspect of human existence, and its influence can be especially profound in family life. During the last decade or so, many writers like R. D. Laing and David Cooper have highlighted the

2. Olthuis, James H. *I Pledge You My Troth* (Harper & Row, 1975) p. 85

more disruptive elements in family life and have even argued towards the death of the family. Dr. Edmund Leach summed up views like these when he described the family as 'the basis of all our discontents'.[3] However, many Christians and non-Christians alike see the family as a gateway to life rather than a prison of restriction. Such people would probably side with the Archbishop of Canterbury in his Call to the Nation when he said, "Give us strong, happy, disciplined families and we shall be well on the way to a strong nation".

MARITAL BREAKDOWN

Reluctantly and inevitably we have to turn our thoughts away from the chatter of children's voices back to the husband and wife, to consider the matters of marital stress and marital breakdown. As has already been argued marriage is difficult, and wherever there is marital bliss there is bound to be marital stress too. It was interesting to see what side effects the series of talks, on which this book is based, had. During those five intensive weeks, Joy and I experienced a degree of marital stress while my head was bent over the books in the study and she coped with the noises off. Sad to relate, and not significantly I hope, this was the first time that I had been oblivious of St. Valentine's day, until I had a card from Joy!

Before we look at this subject more closely, I would like to make a few observations on the so-called danger periods of marriage from the point of view of stress and possible breakdown.

TIMES OF STRESS

The First Years. When you stop and think about it, it is almost incredible that two individuals with many differences, both known and unknown, actually choose to live together for the rest of their lives! After the honeymoon period, the sheer impact of taking someone else into consideration in all the details of life can be quite shattering.

One has heard phrases like, "So-and-so should *never* have married; he's too selfish", and there is no doubt that people do not change simply because they have a marriage certificate. The single man who is cynical, will make a cynical husband; the single woman who has a bad temper will make a bad-tempered wife.

With such drastic adjustments to make, it should not surprise

3. Leach, Edmund. Reith Lectures, 1967

us that a high proportion of marriages that break down begin to do so in the first year or two of living together.

Arrival of Children. We have already considered this from the point of view of the husband who feels shouldered aside by the degree of attention showered on the new arrival. Conversely, the wife who has begun to doubt her husband's love for her may feel even further removed from him at the arrival of the first baby. The newcomer demands her attention and the husband seems content to become more aloof towards her.

Seven-Year Itch. The 'Seven-Year Itch' is a bit of a music hall joke, but the phrase points to the reality of a difficult period in many marriages. After five to ten years of marriage, a husband may find his tired, overworked, often overweight, distracted wife less appealing and, selfishly, his eyes, his mind and his feet may wander elsewhere.

His wife may be distressed by her sullen, moody husband who is out all day and then in front of the telly or out at the pub in the evening. She may find the attentions of a male admirer not only flattering but compelling.

It is important to realise that this over-involvement with a third party may take many different forms. For example, the response may be to a more interesting person, to someone with a special need, or to a friend who makes the wandering spouse feel loved and wanted. In time, the desire for the intruder may lead to full sexual involvement with all its sorry consequences.

Children Leave Home. It is natural to have a great interest in one's children and to long for them to have successful marriages and worthwhile futures, and it can be very difficult to let them go. I remember a girl in her early twenties who, after a great battle, was reluctantly allowed by her possessive mother to buy a dress by herself for the first time.

So often the fear of letting children go is the fear of the long years ahead, perhaps thirty or forty of them, for a husband/ wife relationship that has already become stale and boring. One old dear summed up the later years of her marriage with these words: "He's a very good husband. There's nothing he wouldn't do for me, except talk to me. He just lives for his cacti."

REASONS FOR STRESS

These observations have been sketchy, and the deeper questions remain. Why is it that most marriages survive these milestones without breaking down? How many of these are grimly enduring a 'hell on earth'? Why is it that so many marriages do break up? Are these simply the honest and realistic ones?

Jack Dominian in his excellent book *Marital Breakdown* writes about these areas with great insight. He points out that marital difficulties often relate to where a spouse is chosen to supply vital personal needs which have been lacking in the person's own emotional and psychological development. This point should be made clearer as we consider three main personality problems which often contribute to serious marital stress, separation and even divorce.

Dependency. A failure to achieve a minimum of emotional independence is one of the main causes of marital breakdown. In the chapter on counselling adolescents we saw how certain parents delay the growth towards maturity of their teenage offspring. Independence is specially threatened where parents are habitually anxious or unduly authoritarian.

For the over-anxious parent everything is the subject of worried concern. We may have a scene like this: "Now, Johnny, are you sure you'll be all right? You know how Mummy and Daddy worry about you. Leave your gloves on the radiator a little longer so you won't catch cold. We expect you back at exactly five o'clock. If you're late, you know I shall expect the

OVER-ANXIOUS
PARENTS

OVER-ANXIOUS
MARRIAGE

worst." It is not surprising that Johnny grows up to regard the world as a very anxiety-provoking place. He has always been over-protected and so finds it very hard to carve out an independent existence as a man. He is in danger of always being 'Mum's little boy' and the challenge of marriage will be a threat to his personal survival!

Similarly, over-authoritarian parents can undermine their children's future independence. We saw in chapter two how the children of strict, regimenting, authoritarian parents may become either mealy-mouthed conformists, or rebels. Very often there is a mixed response in which the submissive child later becomes an angry adult, hostile towards the parents.

We can see two main patterns of marriage which may arise from this background of a suppressed childhood.

As we have seen, where such over-protected or over-regimented children reach adulthood still lacking emotional independence and then marry, the marriage will be one of severe stresses. Let us look at three variations on this theme:

(i) *Lean-To Marriages.* Like tends to attract like, and so often two people with great emotional needs gravitate to each other. He may have been over-protected and is looking for someone warm and mothering. He may at first appear strong and confident to her, but this is only a mask and all her neurotic needs are in for a shaking when she finds out what he is really like. As they see each other in a truer light, the insecurities begin to show. She may have a great dread of being alone and need constant reassurance of his love. He too is seeking comfort and yet may find her attentions too smothering in time. As a result, he stays out more and more and she feels more and more let down. Their great temptation is to have a baby simply to try and cement their tottering relationship.

Such a marriage may well break down within the first five or six years. It may battle on doggedly and it is then likely that one of the partners will mature more quickly than the other. This may present a further crisis-situation in that as one becomes more independent, the other will lean even harder and may eventually be left in a state of collapse.

LEAN-TO MARRIAGES

(ii) *Marriage of Rebels.* Sometimes a marriage takes place between two people who are bursting to escape from the clutches of oppressive parents. As a result, marriages like this are often entered into as soon as possible. At first the couple rejoice in their new found freedom. After a while the one feels threatened and dominated by the other and the fight is on!

MARRIAGE OF REBELS

(iii) *Domination/Submission Marriages.* Here is the attraction of opposites. He may be a domineering, managing person looking for someone who is desperate for security. Along she comes, longing for the sort of protection she always had at home. He takes on the parental role, making vital decisions and sheltering his wife from the world's worries and burdens. In time, the awakening adult within her begins to resent his domination and hostility gradually emerges. A war-game begins in which she criticizes his failures, may encourage others to join

DOMINANCE / SUBMISSION

MARRIAGE OF OPPOSITES

REACTION

WEAKER PARTNER MATURES

in the attack and may well use her trump-card of withholding sex. She may also take to drink and the effect of alcohol may give her Dutch courage in her retaliation. Throughout this fighting back she may mature as a person and the dominant/ submissive balance of the marriage is thrown. There is disharmony and marital breakdown looms on the horizon. The situation, of course, may be reversed with the woman dominant, and this can be equally destructive. She may have been suppressed by a tyrannical father and is determined to marry a·man whom she can keep in his place. As he matures, her childhood fears come back and she may well fight him, resisting his decisions and encouraging their children to take sides against him. He in turn may be driven away, may fall out of love and may find himself in the arms of a woman with whom he can relate as an equal for the first time in his life. Here the marriage is severely threatened and may break with a heavy price to be paid by all parties, not the least being the children.

In both these examples the marriage can be saved if the dominant partner admits his or her own weaknesses, thus meeting the maturing weaker partner half way.

Deprivation. Where childhood and adolescence are starved of love, the rest of adult life may be a relentless seeking after emotional fulfilment. This deprivation of love can result from many factors, including illegitimacy, abandonment, or being sent away from home as a child. It is seen where there is little or no emotional closeness in the family, where a parent has been seriously ill or has died early on with no replacement, or where the parents' marriage is breaking up.

Where two emotionally deprived people marry, both seek warmth and security in the other but tragically neither can give the love they both desire. The insufficiencies of the other are exaggerated while the spouse's own shortcomings are not seen. It is easy in this situation, for a while at least, for the couple to blame their difficulties on a lack of material comfort rather than on a lack of loving. It is easier to point at the cracks in the plaster rather than the cracks in their relationship.

In this situation sex is devalued. She is regarded as frigid and withdrawn, and he is seen as the exploiter, using his wife selfishly.

The danger for both parties is that of believing that somewhere else there is someone who can fulfil all needs. Again, a marriage like this may collapse finally following an extramarital affair by either, or both spouses.

DEPRIVATION

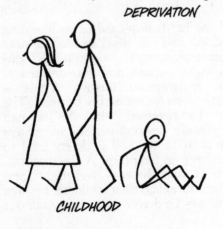

CHILDHOOD

ADOLESCENCE

MARRIAGE   MARITAL BREAKDOWN

Self-Esteem. In a child's earliest years it is specially important that mother and father are available and that basically they approve of the product of their union! If the child's basic needs are disapproved of, then he or she may grow up feeling 'bad' for needing things. This feeling of being unworthy of love may persist into adult life and jeopardise marriage. Jack Dominian quotes a woman who said, "I am surrounded by a husband who adores me, two lovely affectionate children and yet I can enjoy neither because I don't feel I deserve it."[4]

The background of such feelings can be where a child is seen as awkward, backward or of the wrong sex. Again, a child may be rejected because he or she shows those characteristics that the parent despises in himself or herself. Furthermore, a parent's frustrated ambitions can burden a child so that he or she feels bad within for not fulfilling mother's or father's dreams.

Where self-esteem is very low, marriage can take on many different patterns of potential stress. These, illustrated below, include:

(i) Idealising the spouse, where the attention is shifted from the one who feels full of inadequacies to the partner, who is idealised and idolised. This state of affairs may last quite happily until the idol's pedestal begins to show the strain!

(ii) Taking refuge in illness, where the unhappy partner tries to earn affection by being chronically unwell. There may be plenty of attention, but affection itself may wear thin in the face of determined hypochondriasis.

(iii) Preoccupation with self, which may take many forms. In the example shown below, the craving for approval has led to an excessive attention to personal appearance. In effect she is

4. Dominian, J. *Marital Breakdown* (Penguin Books, 1968) p. 62

saying, "I, as a person, am worthless. Please admire my clothes, hair-do and figure instead. It's easier for me that way."

(iv) Serving others frantically, where the insatiable desire for love and acknowledgement leads to a ceaseless round of activity for others. If praise is not given then a feeling of martyrdom creeps in.

I think you will agree that most of us, whether single or married, can find some of these elements in our own lives. How-

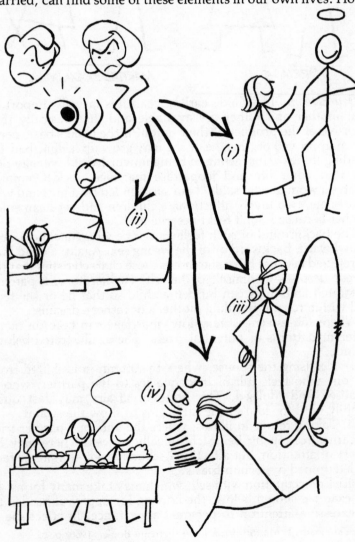

ever, it is where there are serious problems of dependency, deprivation and self-esteem that marriage can be specially threatened.

RECONCILIATION

It has perhaps been depressing to concentrate on some of the key factors in marital breakdown. Let us now consider how you and I can help when others come to us in need. Let me say immediately that one does not have to be married in order to help married people. There are single men and women possessing some of the qualities that I outlined in chapter one — qualities of empathy, being non-judgemental, being good listeners, keeping confidences and having a loving persistence — who can help greatly. Others, who have been through divorce, and whose characters have been strengthened by affliction, will also often be able to care for others in their marital difficulties.

However, to balance this point, let me add that we should not get out of our depth. If the marriage problems presented are considerable, it may be wiser for us, with the permission of the couple involved, to seek more experienced advice. There are many sources of potential help although it is amazing how often needy couples have great difficulty in finding them! Ideally, each Christian fellowship should have access to individuals with counselling ability and experience. Caring bodies, both Christian, such as Care and Counsel in London and Crossline in the South-West, and secular, including Marriage Guidance and the Samaritans, may be able to help considerably. The general practitioner concerned may also have a special interest in marital problems and, if not, will probably have access to other professionals with experience in the various relevant psychotherapies.

Keeping in mind that some people's marital difficulties need more expert advice than we can give, what can we do when married friends turn to us for help? Let us think about our response at two main levels:

(a) Immediate Assistance. There may be problems of accommodation, employment or money that need advice and practical help as soon as possible. Interfering friends or relatives may be making the situation much worse and so 'First Aid treatment' is to deal with these well intentioned disrupters. There may be problems of ill health where, for example, pain and insomnia need dealing with by the couple's doctor before deeper issues can be considered.

(b) Long-term Help. As I commented in the last chapter this is exhaustingly worthwhile, but one must be prepared for a long haul. When you think of the sort of situations we have just considered you will no doubt see that our aims must be modest. We must not expect to revolutionise a marriage into the union of the century! We saw the dangers of such idealism in chapter four. Our ambition for reconciliation must be realistic. In a sentence, we might say with Jack Dominian that 'marital reconciliation ultimately depends on the ability of the spouses to change sufficiently to meet each other's minimal needs'.[5]

This will need great patience while the painful changes take place, where emotional growth can reduce an immature dependence, where emotional deprivation can learn to accept the care and love of others and where self-rejection can diminish while self-reliance increases.

Ultimately, needy persons are helped to discover their own value and their capacity to give themselves in love to others. Instead of the vicious circle of immaturity leading to marital disharmony and this in turn leading to further immature reactions, we are seeking to help our married friends to a new constructive circle. Here emotional growth encourages marital harmony and so the attuned couple matures further, both individually and in relation to each other.

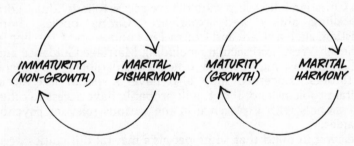

IMMATURITY (NON-GROWTH)   *MARITAL DISHARMONY*   *MATURITY (GROWTH)*   *MARITAL HARMONY*

THE THREE VOIDS

It may be helpful to consider divorce, bereavement and retirement under the general heading of 'The Three Voids' in order to emphasise the feeling of loss and emptiness which may characterise each state. Whether it is the loss of marriage, the loss of a loved one or the loss of a life-time's employment, each of these crises can leave one in a featureless void, where the old, familiar landmarks of life are lost.

5. Dominian, J. op. cit. p. 61

DIVORCE AND REMARRIAGE

Divorce has been around a long time! Jerome quotes the case of a woman in the ancient world who was married to her twenty-third husband, she being his twenty-first wife. Of ancient Rome, Seneca said, "Women are married to be divorced and divorced to be married."

When we turn to the Bible for guidance on the question of divorce, we see first that divorce was *not* part of the original order of creation. Before the Fall, marriage was to involve leaving, cleaving and 'one flesh' for *life*. Secondly, in Deuteronomy 24 we read that divorce was permitted under the Mosaic law where 'a man has found some indecency in his wife'. Thirdly, by New Testament times there were two main schools of thought amongst the Jewish experts on divorce. One group taught that women could be divorced for almost any reason, interpreting 'some indecency in her' very widely. A more conservative school taught that sexual unfaithfulness was the only grounds for divorce.

We need to understand our Lord's words on divorce against the background of these three points. In Matthew 19:8-9 we read that Jesus said to the Pharisees, "For your hardness of heart Moses allowed you to divorce your wives, but from the beginning it was not so. And I say to you: whoever divorces his wife, except for unchastity, and marries another, commits adultery." From this we might accept that divorce is sometimes permissible for man in his fallen state. Jesus points to adultery, the breaking of the 'one flesh' commitment, as the only grounds for divorce. This does not mean that adultery in marriage should automatically lead to divorce. Where there is repentance and forgiveness, there can be a new beginning. We have a strong precedent in our Lord's compassionate handling of the woman taken in adultery, to whom he said, "Go and sin no more" (John 8:11).

In 1 Corinthians 7:15 there seems to be another basis for divorce, that is where a non-Christian spouse is determined to break a marriage, then the Christian is free to remarry.[6]

In many ways divorce today is a scandal. In the UK in 1975 there were over 120,000 divorces. It is interesting to contrast this with the year 1858, the first year following the Matrimonial Causes Act, when there were only 24 divorces. Many of Thomas Hardy's novels dwell on the tragic marriages endured in the days of more stringent divorce laws, whereas today's

6. For stimulating articles on biblical teaching about marriage and divorce, see: Wenham, Gordon, in *Third Way*, 1977 Vol. 1, nos. 20-22
    Job, John, in *Third Way*, 1977, Vol. 1, no. 22

writing sees divorce as the order of the matrimonial day. The pendulum has swung too far.

In trying to counsel others whose marriages are moving towards final breakdown, I believe that we should do all we can to save the marriage in the way already described. However, there will be occasions from time to time when a marriage is not only broken down but seems to be irretrievably dead. On rare occasions, Christians may have to face the fact that theirs is a marriage that God did *not* join together. An example of this exceptional situation can be found in the article quoted on page 81. That particular marriage was dead with the wife living adulterously, and so divorce was the outcome. However, by God's grace, reconciliation *can* be achieved if both spouses are willing.

What of remarriage following divorce? Basically, there seems to be no absolute reason for forbidding this, although many Christian traditions have done so. Tasker, in his commentary on Matthew 19 is very helpful in clarifying the issues. These words of Olthuis are also relevant:

'Remarriage does raise difficult matters. Divorced people have experienced failure in one important part of their lives. They frequently have strong feelings of guilt, shame and anger. Such people need help and understanding so that they can grow personally and avoid making the same mistakes again. Growth is essential, for unless divorced people acknowledge their part in the previous breakdown and show evidence that things will be different a second time, they have no reason to expect that a second marriage will be any better than the first. They should not remarry unless they genuinely try to understand what went wrong, why it went wrong, and why reconciliation attempts failed'.[7]

As Christians who care, our love for friends who have recently been through a divorce needs to be specially sensitive. Old wounds are still open and feelings will be very confused at first. As time goes by, our divorced friend will want to pick up the threads of daily life. It is tragic where people allow a stigma to stick so that a divorcee is not asked out to parties and meals, is feared as a potential man-hunter and, worst of all, is excluded from Christian fellowship. Practical help in financial matters and in child-minding should also have a priority in our caring.

As just outlined we may find that we are in a position of helping a divorced friend, or we may ourselves experience the pain of an irretrievably broken marriage. Either way, it is essential that we try to keep old friendships. However this could be difficult as many friends would be common to both partners.

7. Olthuis, James H. op. cit. p. 71

Further, those involved in the lives of divorced people often feel strong and conflicting emotions, such as anger, rejection and profound disappointment. Friends often side with one spouse or the other, frequently without much understanding of the real issues that led to the marital breakdown. In spite of these difficulties the key to future stability for the divorcees will lie in maintained, loving friendships. In time old wounds should heal, and new friendships with both sexes can enrich life further.

BEREAVEMENT

A marriage that leads to divorce may at first bring relief, but eventually there is often a feeling of emptiness. Bereavement too can bring release to start with if the terminal illness has been long and painful, but sooner or later, especially if the marriage has been a happy one, there will be an aching void. Such a grief reaction will often last in its most acute form beyond the anniversary of the death of the loved one and may commonly be of about eighteen months' duration. If for any reason the spouse finds it difficult to accept a grieving process, then there can be a long-drawn-out state of determined silence on the subject of the dead husband or wife for years, or even decades.

C. S. Lewis's book, *A Grief Observed*, is a masterpiece of soul-searching honesty on this subject. As you may know, he married late in life and was supremely happy in his short-lived marriage. His wife, stricken by cancer, seems to have been snatched from him at the prime of their beautiful relationship. Realistically, he traces the varied ways of feeling he experienced following her death. He starts by saying, 'No one ever told me that grief felt so like fear. I am not afraid, but the sensation is like being afraid. The same fluttering in the stomach, the same restlessness, the yawning'.[8] He then moves on to agonise with God about the death of his beloved wife. If you want to be able to care for a friend who is bereaved, I would recommend this book for careful reading.

In our caring for such, we should heed T. S. Eliot's words, 'Teach us to care and not to care. Teach us to sit still.'[9] Words may bring little comfort whereas a good hug will. Time will be needed for our friend to work through his or her grief. It is so tempting to advise this or that activity, "to take their mind off it" we say. We should resist this temptation. Solitude may be desired and a good friend will allow it. Weeping, angry outbursts and the off-loading of worries will all help.

8. Lewis, C. S. *A Grief Observed* (Faber and Faber, 1961), p. 7
9. Eliot, T. S. *Ash-Wednesday, part I. Collected Poems* (Faber & Faber, 1936)

In time there will be the need for increasing activity again. At first this will be the everyday things, avoiding heavy responsibility, rather as Simon Peter did when he said, "I am going fishing", after the death of Jesus (John 21:3).

Generally, it will be best for the bereaved person to stay in familiar surroundings amongst friends, where memories of the loved one can be restored. Ultimately, especially in the case of a young widow or widower, there may be remarriage. It is important to see such a desire as a compliment to the first marriage!

RETIREMENT

Not only divorce and bereavement, but also retirement can be a void for many people. The tired housewife in this poem longed for her void.

> Here lies a poor woman who was always tired,
> She lived in a house where help wasn't hired:
> Her last words on earth were: "Dear friends, I am going
> To where there's no cooking or washing or sewing,
> For everything there is exact to my wishes,
> For where they don't eat there's no washing of dishes.
> I'll be where loud anthems will always be ringing,
> But having no voice I'll be quit of the singing.
> Don't mourn for me now, don't mourn for me never.
> I am going to do nothing for ever and ever."[10]

Many women, engulfed by routine housework, would echo this poem with its prospect of doing 'nothing for ever and ever'.

For such women, whether married or unmarried, the idea of retirement can be a myth. In our counselling we should remember that the tedium of domestic chores can be not only backbreaking but depressing. We may need to encourage the sharing of these burdens with others, such as a retired husband, other relatives, or, where appropriate, friends of the ageing women whom one is trying to help.

Many women, both married and single, do of course go out to work and may therefore face similar problems of adjustment on retirement as men do. However, with their wider interests and greater experience of home-making, many of these women seem to cope better than most men on retirement. So many men, on finishing work for the last time, become inward and

10. Anon. 'On a Tired Housewife.' *The Penguin Book of Comic and Curious Verse* (Penguin Books, 1952), p. 31

backward looking like the one in Steve Turner's poem, 'Life Begins at Forty and Closes Early':

> At some point in his life
> there came a shortage
> of future.
> At some point in his life
> the past became more certain,
> more reliable.
> It was then they called him old.
> It was then they bought him
> a wooden chair to live in
> and a window to look out of.
> When he became hungry
> he thought of meals
> he'd once eaten.
> When he was lonely
> he imagined a friend.
> When he was depressed
> he remembered an adventure.
> He lived in his chair
> and grew fat on the past.[11]

Frequently, men have reached a peak in their job as far as experience and respect are concerned by the time they retire at sixty or sixty-five. Their fear of retirement is so often due to a loss of status. For all their working days their identity has been tied up with their particular firm, trade, business or profession. Suddenly — they feel nobody!

It is surely wise to think ahead, not just from the point of view of superannuation and insurance schemes. Life will be much richer if hobbies and interests and a wide circle of friends are developed in one's forties and fifties, rather than by waiting till sixty-five to take up golf, grow chrysanthemums or buy a pair of binoculars and start bird-watching.

These words of Sister Phoebe, quoted by Margaret Evening, seem to touch the right note for facing retirement and old age:

'The time comes to most of us when, whether we like it or not, old age and failing powers force us into solitude. Many people dread this time, and of course we can't relapse into laziness and become increasingly a burden to others — we must keep going while we can. But inevitably we shall become more and more alone. If we have longed for solitude, and learned to live it because we find God there, it should be that the last years of a long life will be the happiest of all, lived so close to Him

11. Turner, Steve. 'Life Begins at Forty and Closes Early, part I.' *Tonight We Will Fake Love* (Charisma Books, 1974) p. 42

that His life and love can shine through us to bless countless souls.'[12]

FOR FURTHER READING

Dominian, J. _Marital Breakdown_ (London, Penguin Books Ltd.) 1968
Grams, A. _Changes in Family Life_ (Cambridge, Concordia Publishing House) 1968
Lewis, C. S. _A Grief Observed_ (London, Faber & Faber) 1961
Schaeffer, E. _What is a Family?_ (London, Hodder & Stoughton) 1976
Tournier, Paul _Marriage Difficulties_ (London, SCM Press) 1967
Townsend, A. _Families without Pretending_ (London, The Scripture Union) 1976

12. Evening, Margaret. _Who Walk Alone_ (Hodder and Stoughton, 1974) p. 182

CHAPTER SIX

Conclusion

In chapter one I asked the question, 'What is the aim of counselling?' We then looked at Ephesians 4 and saw that the restored image of God in our lives, i.e. Christian maturity, is the eventual aim. Whether we prefer other phrases such as pastoral concern or simply helping others by counselling or Christian caring, our desire is the same: to encourage those around us towards this goal of completeness through Christ.

This is neither a handbook on evangelism, proclaiming the Good News of salvation, nor on social action, emphasising the environmental and communal needs of people. It is, however, an attempt to show something of the counsel of God in the areas of singleness, marriage and family life. Counselling, as defined in chapter one, rubs shoulders with both evangelism and social concern, but it is a pity to be too rigorous in dividing one from another. The heart of the 'whole counsel of God' for needy men and women is the restoring of their relationship with him through the finished work of his Son. This is no narrow concept! God's rightful place is as Lord of the entire created order, including *every* aspect of man's individual and corporate life. The evangelist, the counsellor, and any Christian working to improve social conditions have the same ultimate concerns and their activity should dovetail and, at times, overlap. None should forget the full spectrum of need — spiritual, psychological, emotional, physical and communal — that all men and women have, although a person's difficulties may be primarily in one area or another at any point in time. All three activities should be motivated by love for God and for our fellow men and women, seeking to meet the needs of the whole man.

We have looked at the needs and hopes of Shakespeare's 'seven ages' of man; we have considered psychological and emotional adjustments and maladjustments 'from the womb to the tomb', seeking to clarify scriptural principles throughout.

Let us conclude this book where we began, in Ephesians, by considering the last part of chapter 4 and the first two verses of chapter 5. As we read these words we should remember that, whether we are single, married, divorced or widowed; whether we have a strong sense of identity or a weak one; whether we are floundering towards maturity or whether we can thank God for some growth in that direction; we are all, if we have opened ourselves to Christ, members of a family marked by self-giving love, the 'household of God'.

'Therefore, putting away falsehood, let every one speak the truth with his neighbour, for we are members one of another.

'Be angry but do not sin; do not let the sun go down on your anger, and give no opportunity to the devil.

'Let the thief no longer steal, but rather let him labour, doing honest work with his hands, so that he may be able to give to those in need.

'Let no evil talk come out of your mouths, but only such as is good for edifying, as fits the occasion, that it may impart grace to those who hear.

'And do not grieve the Holy Spirit of God, in whom you were sealed for the day of redemption.

'Let all bitterness and wrath and anger and clamour and slander be put away from you, with all malice.

'And be kind to one another, tenderhearted, forgiving one another, as God in Christ forgave you.

'Therefore be imitators of God, as beloved children.

'And walk in love, as Christ loved us and gave himself up for us, a fragrant offering and sacrifice to God.'

FOR FURTHER READING

Harris, T.A. *I'm OK, You're OK* (Pan Books) 1973
Hooper, D. & Roberts, J. *Disordered Lives* (London, Marriage Guidance Council) 1973
Sheehy, G. *Passages* (London, Corgi Books) 1977